GREAT
POEMS *for*
GRAND
CHILDREN

GREAT POEMS *for* GRAND CHILDREN

○

Edited by Celestine Frost

Drawings by Brian Cronin

AARP STERLING

New York / London
www.sterlingpublishing.com

AARP Books publishes a wide range of titles on health, personal finance, lifestyle, and other subjects to enrich the lives of 50+ Americans. For more information, go to www.aarp.org/books.

AARP, established in 1958, is a nonprofit organization with more than 40 million members age 50 and older. The views expressed herein do no necessarily represent the policies of AARP and should not be construed as endorsements.

The AARP name and logo are registered trademarks of AARP, used under license to Sterling Publishing Co., Inc.

STERLING and the distinctive Sterling logo are registered trademarks of Sterling Publishing Co., Inc.

Library of Congress Cataloging-in-Publication Data

Great poems for grand children / edited by Celestine Frost.
p. cm.
ISBN 978-1-4027-2512-8
1. Children's poetry, English. 2. Children's poetry, American.
3. English poetry. 4. American poetry. I. Frost, Celestine.
PR1175.3.G74 2010
821.008'09282--dc22
2008043105

2 4 6 8 10 9 7 5 3 1

Published by Sterling Publishing Co., Inc.
387 Park Avenue South, New York, N.Y. 10016
Copyright © 2010 by AARP

Manufactured in China
All rights reserved

Sterling ISBN 978-1-4027-2512-8

Creative Director: Carl Lehman-Haupt
Artist: Brian Cronin
Page Layout: Antje Kharchi

For information about custom editions, special sales, premium and corporate purchases, please contact Sterling Special Sales Department at 800-805-5489 or specialsales@sterlingpublishing.com.

for

Holt and Dmitri, Olivia and Sasha,
Keene and Peter and Audrey,
and Jamee and Chance.
And in memory of Grumps.
And for Steve Magnusson, whose love of poetry
and his "shining armor" made him my ideal editor —
wherever he may be.

○

"BOYS AND GIRLS COME OUT TO PLAY,
THE MOON DOTH SHINE AS BRIGHT AS DAY."

Contents

◎

Illustrations XVIII

Preface XX

I Nursery Rhymes, Tongue Twisters & Nonsense Verses

II My Home

III Bedtime

IV Friends & School

V Animal Friends

VI Seasons of the Year

VII Fairies, Witches, Goblins & Company

VIII Wise Words

IX My Country

X Travel

XI True Love

XII Creator & Creation

XIII Seasons of Life

XIV Heroes

Illustrations

○

PAINTINGS BY BRIAN CRONIN

"You cannot depend
on your eyes
when your imagination
is out of focus."
— MARK TWAIN

PREFACE

◎

THE IMAGINATION

My seven-year-old grandson can see hobbits. This is not easy, for the hobbit, a cozy homebody without much in the way of magical powers, does have the ability to vanish just before the human eye can fall upon him. My grandson, however, is so stealthy, so patient, and so swift he could give lessons to a cat; he has actually seen many hobbits and can describe them. With equal ease, still in the kingdom of the imagination, he and I discuss Peter Russell's model of the atom, magnified to the size of a football stadium, where the electrons are "like peas flying around the stands."

My grandson may one day relinquish his belief in mythological beings and adapt to the dictates of conventional understanding as he reacts to the skepticism of his older friends; but, as of now, he is a person whose imagination is in focus.

THE MOON

If, as the great linguist Wilhelm von Humboldt says, language is the organ of thought, might poetry be considered the organ of the imagination? And its symbol be . . . *the moon?* It is the moon that pulls the sea, the mysterious and mighty sea, and tugs at the imagination.

Look through these pages, please, taking note of the moon and some the actions in these poems inspired by it.

A cow jumps over it
An old woman is tossed up to it in a basket
The old baboon by the light of the moon is combing his golden hair
A baby seal sleeps while his mother sings him a seal lullaby
And Paul Revere, "a shape in the moonlight," gallops through history
An angel writes in a book of gold
"When only the still moon rages" Dylan Thomas writes a poem
And a scared little rabbit comes into his own as "king of the ghosts"
A savvy nymph steals the moon's beads
Witches cast their spells
And, of course, the fairy folk run wild

As for the owl and the pussy cat, "they danced by the light of the moon, the moon, they danced by the light of the moon."

And, in the very first poem of this anthology, where "the moon doth shine as bright as day!" boys and girls are summoned out to play in its glory, to leap their limits and give free rein to the Imagination.

◦

GREAT POEMS FOR GRAND CHILDREN

Most of the poems in this anthology were chosen especially for young children who are, even by the light of the moon, expected to age. They continue in its sights long after they sit in grandpa's lap reading "Hey, diddle, diddle, the cat in the fiddle." Above all the great and nourishing connection between grandparent and grandchild, between innocence and wisdom, is held in sostenuto throughout.

But there are poems for older children and for grandparents, too. Some of these can also be enjoyed by a younger child with a little grandparental preparation. There is, for instance, the poem I have just mentioned, "A Rabbit as King of the Ghosts," which a literal-minded reader may find baffling. But if it is seen, from the beginning, as a poem for anyone who has ever been bullied, it becomes easy to understand and highly satisfying to read aloud . Of course, *the reader must become the rabbit,* must find, in his or her own memory, a time of oppression and the relief of freedom from it. This is a great dramatic soliloquy, celebrating victory over one's enemy. I hope all readers will give it a try. It is a psalm of triumph, a tribute to the moon and the marvelous influence of its light, which stills the oppressor and releases the powers of the imagination.

And if the reader has yet to experience the freedom of which the rabbit tells, it is highly recommended that he or she go outside some night and sit, for an hour or two, alone, beneath the moon.

There are other poems about which the reader should be alerted. "Little Orphant Annie" is one of them. This marvelous, enduring classic is really scary and should not be read at bedtime!

In fact, no poem with which the reader is not familiar should ever be read aloud to a child. To do a poem justice, it must be studied and rehearsed. This is not only because of its possible difficulty or its (possibly unwelcome) subject matter, but also because all poems contain surprises and, as Walter de la Mare says, "even the simplest ones have secrets which will need a pretty close searching out."

Among the poems that may pose a dilemma for the grandparent are two immortal poems about death. John Donne's "Death Be Not Proud" is a charming, sassy poem in which the poet teases and thumbs his nose at Death. And then there is Dylan Thomas. I will never forget the twelve-year-old who climbed to the lectern at his father's funeral and recited, with all the thunder his young voice could summon, "Do Not Go Gentle into That Good Night." In an anthology for grandchildren and grandparents, these poems have a place.

There are other poems, especially in the latter half of the book, that were not intended for children but that are about children and are,

I think, of special value in this anthology in that they address a human being's deepest fears—fears that are accepted, even welcomed, and, somehow, turned inside out through the imaginative powers of a child.

In "The Day Millicent Found the World," for instance, Millicent goes, every morning, deeper and deeper into the forest, until one day, she knew: "Lost. *She had achieved a mysterious world*" (italics mine). Why does Millicent challenge herself like this? Is it in pursuit of her independence? Is this a poem about growing up? In "Something That Happens Right Now," again the child goes out alone and revels in his fears of abandonment.

These poems may come as a shock to a child who, discovering in them a description of his or her most private behavior, may feel found out. For these poems are descriptions of a kind of vision quest—or rite of initiation—as instinctively devised by the child whose fears of isolation are transformed by "the power of longing" into a transcendent experience.

As for the adult who reads these poems alone or with a child, may the awareness of this power, perhaps long forgotten, be renewed!

And in such ways, may this anthology be useful to us grandparents as we clarify our thoughts about just what our intellectual and emotional legacy will be. Some of the poems we grandparents may wish to read alone in order to think about this legacy are among the greatest poems in all our literature. These pull us into the depths of our being—that mysterious and mighty ocean into which we do not often venture—from which we will emerge into our workaday lives with new insights, wiser and refreshed. (Do not miss the cluster of animal poems at the end of Section V that includes "A Blessing" and "The Fish.")

◎

ABOUT THIS BOOK

The poems have been organized into 14 sections to reflect a child's gradual penetration of the world. The arc of the book begins intimately at home and expands outward to include the nation and its heroes and history. In this scheme, My Home, Bedtime, and Animal Friends broaden to become My Country, Travel, and Creator and Creation. "Nonsense" takes a giant leap of the imagination to become "Wise Words" while "Friends and School" evolves into "True Love"—as this little epigraph from Romeo and Juliet so neatly puts it:

Love goes toward love as schoolboys from their books.
But love from love toward school with heavy looks.

These connections form a kind of cat's cradle, stretching across the sections and pulling them into a whole.

◎

BLACK ELK

As a child of nine, Black Elk, a Sioux Indian, received a great vision. This vision could, he believed, save his people and their way of life (which was fast being destroyed). If he could tell it to all nations, it might even save the world. All his life Black Elk has borne the responsibility of this vision, unable to find a way to express it. Now, approaching the end of his life, and fearing the wrath of the "Six Grandfathers" from whom he long ago received this vision, he goes up into the hills and cries out to them in despair: "A pitiful old man you see me here, and I have fallen away and done nothing."

It was at about this time that Black Elk was found by a poet who could transcribe his words. This story (which rivals the Book of Revelations in splendor) has by now been translated into many languages. Many of us, in the later years of our lives, may also feel we are the bearers of some message and may be distressed at having failed to deliver it. So much so that one might think of the transmission of this legacy as the urgent task of old age. But . . . what, *exactly,* is it I want to say? Like the hobbit, who vanishes just before the human eye can fall upon him, just before I find the words to express "my wisdom," it scoots away!

Once, a toddling child and I came upon a small blue wasp who, with tremendous effort, was lugging a cicada many times her size across rough ground. When we later researched the blue wasp's ways, we learned that she had paralyzed the cicada and was dragging it to her larval chamber so that her larvae, when they hatched, would have something fresh and delicious to munch upon. I have the same instinct—an irrepressible urge to stuff the brains of my descendants with live (nay! immortal) food.

But a child's interest is a wild thing, as wild as any hawk or humming-bird, and not easy to catch. It is not easy to stuff poems into a child. The timing must be good, the bait select, and the presentation irresistible.

○

WORDS OF WISDOM

"I wish I had some words of wisdom for you," my father said, realizing that, though he was only sixty-six his time had come to die. "Gosh, Daddy!" I protested, "your *example*!" He loved poetry, and his appreciation for exact-ness in speech occupied him up to the end. He scoured his memory for poems that could engage his mind and for words that nailed his feelings. Each time I came to see him in the hospital, he sent me home with an assignment: *Flaccid:* are the *cs* soft (like the meaning of the word) as in *placid*? Or are they hard as in *account*? Can you find Macbeth's despairing speech that begins "Tomorrow and tomorrow and tomorrow" and ends "full of sound and fury, signifying nothing"?

My children were too young to really know their grandfather, and he too ill in his last years to enjoy them. Added to his illness was his dismay at the direction things were taking. "Progress" had caught up with us on our small farm surrounded by marsh and virgin woods. A thousand-year-old oak in our vicinity had been casually torn out to make room for a "convenience store." Forests were being felled and fields paved over. The disappearance of the delicate china-back fiddler crab and the muck that had replaced the sandy bottom told of a polluted marsh. The world that he loved, like Black Elk's world a hundred years earlier, was being destroyed. Even television, which had seemed nothing more than an in-nocent diversion at first, now proved a poor substitute for passionate discussions in the moonlight on the porch or reading aloud. And when the evening program ended, my father would turn the TV off and herd us all outside to check up on the stars as if, with a click of the knob, we might refocus the imagination.

THESE POEMS

I was just four when my own grandfather died, and I wept and wept. My father bundled me into the car and took me for a long drive across bridges and past fields where cows and horses grazed and a newborn foal struggled to its feet but could not console me. And he bought me an ice cream cone, which I refused. But that night, as I lay awake in the inky dark, Grumps appeared! He was dressed in his three-piece salt and pepper suit, as always, with his watch and chain, his hat and cane, and he came floating down from heaven toward me on a pair of gossamer pink wings and bearing an enormous bouquet.

And here it is! this anthology, a collection of poems—or, rather, a collection of flowers (for that is what the word *anthology* means if you take it back to the Greek). Each poem in this collection has a "message." But the real subject here is *poetry*—poetry itself; for a poem, though made of words, says more than words can express. It is as if the words of the poem, in just that combination, had a special chemistry from which there rose—as from a flower—a kind of metaphysical perfume that nourishes the imagination and, in the case of those who read the poems aloud together, as we hope grandparents and grandchildren will, transmits a secret wisdom as no ordinary language can.

GREAT POEMS *for* GRAND CHILDREN

TO BRUSH THE COBWEBS OFF THE SKY!

I

Nursery Rhymes,
Tongue Twisters,
& Nonsense Verses

A little nonsense now and then
Is relished by the wisest men.
—ANONYMOUS

BOYS AND GIRLS COME OUT TO PLAY
OLD NURSERY RHYME

Boys and girls come out to play,
The moon doth shine as bright as day,
Leave your supper and leave your sleep,
And join your playfellows in the street.
Come with a whoop and come with a call,
Come with a good will or not at all;
Up the ladder and down the wall,
You bring a hoop and I'll bring a ball,
I'll bring a dream and you bring a song,
And we'll frolic in the moonlight all night long!

◎

THERE WAS AN OLD WOMAN
OLD NURSERY RHYME

There was an old woman tossed up in a basket,
Seventeen times as high as the moon;
Where she was going I couldn't but ask it,
For in her hand she carried a broom.

Old woman, old woman, old woman, quoth I,
Where are you going to up so high?
To brush the cobwebs off the sky!
May I go with you? Aye, by and by.

HEY DIDDLE, DIDDLE

OLD NURSERY RHYME

Hey diddle, diddle,
The cat and the fiddle,
The cow jumped over the moon.
The little dog laughed
To see such sport
And the dish ran away with the spoon.

◎

I HAD A LITTLE NUT TREE

I had a little nut tree,
Nothing would it bear
But a silver nutmeg
And a golden pear.

The king of Spain's daughter
Came to visit me
And all for the sake
Of my little nut tree.

I skipped over land,
I skipped over sea,
And all the birds in the air
Couldn't catch me.

◎

LITTLE JACK HORNER

Little Jack Horner
Sat in a corner,
Eating his Christmas pie;
He put in his thumb
And pulled out a plum,
And said, "What a good boy am I!"

Diddle, diddle dumpling

Diddle, diddle dumpling, my son John
Went to bed with his stockings on;
One shoe off and one shoe on;
Diddle, diddle dumpling, my son John.

◎

There was an owl lived in an oak

There was an owl lived in an oak,
    Wisky, wasky, weedle;
And every word he ever spoke
    Was fiddle, faddle, feedle.

A gunner chanced to come that way,
    Wisky, wasky, weedle;
Says he, I'll shoot you, silly bird,
    Fiddle, faddle, feedle.

The owl swooped down upon his head,
    Wisky, wasky, weedle;
Snatched off his cap, and laid an egg;
    Fiddle, faddle, feedle.

◎

Pussy cat, pussy cat

Pussy cat, pussy cat,
Where have you been?
I've been to London
To visit the Queen.

Pussy cat, pussy cat,
What did you there?
I frightened a little mouse
Under her chair.

RIDE A COCK HORSE TO BANBURY CROSS

OLD NURSERY RHYME

Ride a cock horse
to Banbury Cross
To see an old lady
Ride on a white horse.

With rings on her fingers
And bells on her toes,
She shall have music
Wherever she goes.

◎

SO, NATURALISTS OBSERVE

JONATHAN SWIFT ON THE INVENTION OF THE MICROSCOPE

So, naturalists observe, a flea
Hath smaller fleas that on him prey
And these have smaller still to bite 'em
And so proceed ad infinitum.

◎

THE THISTLE-SIFTER

She is a thistle-sifter.
She has a sieve of unsifted thistles
and a sieve of sifted thistles
and the sieve of unsifted thistles
she sifts into the sieve of sifted thistles
because she is a thistle-sifter.

HOW MUCH WOOD COULD A WOODCHUCK CHUCK

How much wood could a woodchuck chuck
If a woodchuck could chuck wood?
Just as much as a woodchuck would
If a woodchuck could chuck wood.

◎

PETER PIPER

Peter Piper picked a peck of pickled peppers;
A peck of pickled peppers Peter Piper picked;
If Peter Piper picked a peck of pickled peppers,
Where's the peck of pickled peppers Peter Piper picked?

◎

A FLEA AND A FLY

A flea and a fly got caught in a flue.
    Said the fly, "Let us flee."
    Said the flea, "Let us fly."
So together they flew through a flaw in the flue.

◎

THE SELFISH SHELLFISH

The selfish shellfish
Sits upon a shelf from which
Stealthily he sells fish;
So the other shellfish
Think he is so selfish
That they have no well-wish
For the wealthy, selfish, stealthy shellfish.

HOW DOTH THE LITTLE CROCODILE
LEWIS CARROLL

How doth the little crocodile
   Improve his shining tail,
And pour the waters of the Nile
   On every golden scale!

How cheerfully he seems to grin,
   How neatly spreads his claws,
And welcomes little fishes in
   With gently smiling jaws!

◦

THE THREE LITTLE KITTENS
ELIZA LEE FOLLEN

Three little kittens lost their mittens;
   And they began to cry,
    "Oh, mother dear,
     We very much fear
That we have lost our mittens."

   "Lost your mittens!
    You naughty kittens!
Then you shall have no pie!"
       "Mee-ow, mee-ow, mee-ow."
  "No, you shall have no pie."
       "Mee-ow, mee-ow, mee-ow."

The three little kittens found their mittens;
   And they began to cry,
    "Oh, mother dear,
     See here, see here!
See, we have found our mittens!"

"Put on your mittens,
    You silly kittens,
And you may have some pie."
        "Purr-r, purr-r, purr-r,
Oh, let us have the pie!
        Purr-r, purr-r, purr-r."

The three little kittens put on their mittens,
    And soon ate up the pie;
        "Oh, mother dear,
        We greatly fear
That we have soiled our mittens!"

    "Soiled your mittens!
    You naughty kittens!"
Then they began to sigh,
        "Mee-ow, mee-ow, mee-ow."
Then they began to sigh,
        "Mee-ow, mee-ow, mee-ow."

The three little kittens washed their mittens,
    And hung them out to dry;
        "Oh, mother dear,
        Do not you hear
That we have washed our mittens?"

    "Washed your mittens!
    Oh, you're good kittens!
But I smell a rat close by,
        Hush, hush! Mee-ow, mee-ow."
"We smell a rat close by,
        Mee-ow, mee-ow, mee-ow."

I SAW A SHIP A-SAILING

I saw a ship a-sailing,
A-sailing on the sea;
And oh! It was all laden
With pretty things for thee!

There were comfits in the cabin
And apples in the hold;
The sails were made of silk
And the masts were made of gold.

The four and twenty sailors
That stood between the decks
Were four and twenty white mice
With chains about their necks.

The captain was a duck
With a packet on his back;
And when the ship began to move,
The captain said, "Quack! Quack!"

○

I WENT TO THE ANIMAL FAIR

I went to the animal fair,
The birds and beasts were there.
The big baboon, by the light of the moon,
Was combing his auburn hair.
The monkey, he got drunk,
And sat on the elephant's trunk.
The elephant sneezed and fell on his knees,
And what became of the monk, the monk?
And what became of the monk?

SIX LITTLE MICE SAT DOWN TO SPIN

Six little mice sat down to spin.
Kitty passed by and she peeped in.
What are you doing, my little men?
Weaving coats for gentlemen.
Shall I come in and cut off your threads?
No, no, Mistress Kitty, you'd bite off our heads.
Oh, no, I'll not; I'll help you to spin.
That may be so, but you can't come in.

◎

THERE WAS A CROOKED MAN

There was a crooked man
Who walked a crooked mile.
He found a crooked sixpence
And smiled a crooked smile.
He bought a crooked cat
Which caught a crooked mouse
And they all lived together
In a little crooked house.

◎

SING A SONG OF SIXPENCE

Sing a song of sixpence,
A pocket full of rye;
Four and twenty blackbirds
Baked in a pie.

When the pie was opened
The birds began to sing;
Now wasn't that a dainty dish
To set before the king?

The king was in the counting house
Counting out his money;
The queen was in the parlor
Eating bread and honey.

The maid was in the garden
Hanging out the clothes
When down came a blackbird
And snipped off her nose.

○

JACK AND JILL

Jack and Jill went up the hill
To fetch a pail of water.
Jack fell down and broke his crown
And Jill came tumbling after.

Then up Jack got and off did trot
As fast as he could caper,
To old Dame Dob who patched his nob
With vinegar and brown paper.

○

JACK SPRAT

Jack Sprat could eat no fat,
His wife could eat no lean;
And so betwixt them both, you see,
They licked the platter clean.

OLD KING COLE

OLD NURSERY RHYME

Old King Cole was a merry old soul
    And a merry old soul was he;
He called for his pipe in the middle of the night
    And he called for his fiddlers three.

Every fiddler had a fine fiddle
    And a very fine fiddle had he;
Oh, there's none so rare as can compare
    With King Cole and his fiddlers three

◎

THE MAN IN THE WILDERNESS

The man in the wilderness asked of me,
How many strawberries grew in the sea.
I answered him as I thought good,
"As many red herrings as grow in the wood."

◎

AS I WAS GOING TO ST. IVES

As I was going to St. Ives,
I met a man with seven wives;
Each wife had seven sacks;
Each sack had seven cats;
Each cat had seven kits.
Kits, cats, sacks, and wives,
How many were going to St. Ives?

A PIN HAS A HEAD, BUT HAS NO HAIR
CHRISTINA GEORGINA ROSSETTI

A pin has a head, but has no hair;
A clock has a face, but no mouth there;
Needles have eyes, but they cannot see;
A fly has trunks without lock or key;
A timepiece may lose but cannot win;
A corn-field dimples without a chin;
A hill has no leg, but has a foot;
A wine-glass a stem, but not a root;
A watch has hands, but no thumb or fingers;
A boot has a tongue, but is no singer;
Rivers run, though they have no feet;
A saw has teeth, but it does not eat;
Ash trees have keys, yet never a lock;
And baby crows, without being a cock.

◦

ELETELEPHONY
LAURA E. RICHARDS

Once there was an elephant
Who tried to use the telephant—
No! No! I mean an elephone
Who tried to use the telephone—
(Dear me! I am not certain quite
That even now I've got it right.)

Howe'er it was, he got his trunk
Entangled in the telephunk;
The more he tried to get it free,
The louder buzzed the telephee—
(I fear I'd better drop the song
Of elephop and telephong!)

JABBERWOCKY

LEWIS CARROLL

'Twas brillig, and the slithy toves
Did gyre and gimble in the wabe:
All mimsy were the borogoves,
And the mome raths outgrabe.

"Beware the Jabberwock, my son!
The jaws that bite, the claws that catch!
Beware the Jubjub bird, and shun
The frumious Bandersnatch!"

He took his vorpal sword in hand:
Long time the manxome foe he sought—
So rested he by the Tumtum tree,
And stood a while in thought.

And, as in uffish thought he stood,
The Jabberwock, with eyes of flame,
Came whiffling through the tulgey wood,
And burbled as it came!

One two! One two! And through and through
The vorpal blade went snicker-snack!
He left it dead, and with its head
He went galumphing back.

"And hast thou slain the Jabberwock?
Come to my arms, my beamish boy!
Oh frabjous day! Callooh! Callay!"
He chortled in his joy.

'Twas brillig, and the slithy toves
Did gyre and gimble in the wabe:
All mimsy were the borogoves,
And the mome raths outgrabe.

A Tragic Story

ADELBERT VON CHAMISSO
TRANSLATED BY WILLIAM MAKEPEACE THACKERAY

There lived a sage in days of yore,
And he a handsome pigtail wore;
But wondered much, and sorrowed more,
Because it hung behind him.

He mused upon this curious case,
And swore he'd change the pigtail's place,
And have it hanging at his face,
Not dangling there behind him.

Says he, "The mystery I've found,—
I'll turn me round,"—he turned him round,
But still it hung behind him.

Then round and round, and out and in,
All day the puzzled sage did spin;
In vain—it mattered not a pin—
The pigtail hung behind him.

And right and left, and roundabout,
And up and down and in and out
He turned; but still the pigtail stout
Hung steadily behind him.

And though his efforts never slack,
And though he twist, and twirl, and tack,
Alas! still faithful to his back,
The pigtail hangs behind him.

THE LOBSTER QUADRILLE

LEWIS CARROLL

"Will you walk a little faster?" said a whiting to a snail,
"There's a porpoise close behind us, and he's treading on my tail.
See how eagerly the lobsters and the turtles all advance!
They are waiting on the shingle—will you come and join the dance?
          Will you, won't you, will you, won't you,
               will you join the dance?
          Will you, won't you, will you, won't you,
               won't you join the dance?

"You can really have no notion how delightful it will be
When they take us up and throw us, with the lobsters out to sea!"
But the snail replied, "Too far, too far!" and gave a look askance—
Said he thanked the whiting kindly, but he would not join the dance.
          Would not, could not, would not, could not
               would not join the dance.
          Would not, could not, would not, could not,
               could not join the dance.

"What matters it how far we go?" his scaly friend replied.
"There is another shore, you know, upon the other side.
The further off from England the nearer is to France—
Then turn not pale, beloved snail, but come and join the dance.
          Will you, won't you, will you, won't you,
               will you join the dance?
          Will you, won't you, will you, won't you,
               won't you join the dance?"

THE SONG OF THE JELLICLES

T.S. ELIOT

Jellicle Cats come out tonight
Jellicle Cats come one come all:
The Jellicle Moon is shining bright—
Jellicles come to the Jellicle Ball.

Jellicle Cats are black and white,
Jellicle Cats are rather small;
Jellicle Cats are merry and bright,
And pleasant to hear when they caterwaul.
Jellicle Cats have cheerful faces,
Jellicle Cats have bright black eyes;
They like to practice their airs and graces
And wait for the Jellicle Moon to rise.

Jellicle Cats develop slowly,
Jellicle Cats are not too big;
Jellicle Cats are roly-poly,
They know how to dance a gavotte and a jig.
Until the Jellicle Moon appears
They make their toilette and take their repose:
Jellicles wash behind their ears,
Jellicles dry between their toes.

Jellicle Cats are white and black,
Jellicle Cats are of moderate size;
Jellicles jump like a jumping-jack,
Jellicle Cats have moonlit eyes.
They're quiet enough in the morning hours,
They're quiet enough in the afternoon,
Reserving their terpsichorean powers
To dance by the light of the Jellicle Moon.

Jellicle Cats are black and white,
Jellicle Cats (as I said) are small;
If it happens to be a stormy night
They will practice a caper or two in the hall.
If it happens the sun is shining bright
You would say they had nothing to do at all:
They are resting and saving themselves to be right
For the Jellicle Moon and the Jellicle Ball.

◎

THE TABLE AND THE CHAIR
EDWARD LEAR

I

Said the Table to the Chair,
"You can hardly be aware,
"How I suffer from the heat,
"And from chilblains on my feet!
"If we took a little walk,
"We might have a little talk!
"Pray let us take the air!"
Said the Table to the Chair.

II

Said the Chair unto the Table,
"Now you *know* we are not able!
"How foolishly you talk,
"When you know we *cannot* walk!"
Said the Table, with a sigh,
"It can do no harm to try,
"I've as many legs as you,
"Why can't we walk on two?"

III

So they both went slowly down,
And walked about the town
With a cheerful bumpy sound,
As they toddled round and round.
And everybody cried,
As they hastened to their side,
"See! the Table and the Chair
"Have come out to take the air!"

IV

But in going down an alley,
To a castle in a valley,
They completely lost their way,
And wandered all the day,
Till, to see them safely back,
They paid a Ducky-quack,
And a Beetle, and a Mouse,
Who took them to their house.

V

Then they whispered to each other,
"O delightful little brother!
"What a lovely walk we've taken!
"Let us dine on Beans and Bacon!"
So the Ducky, and the leetle
Browny-Mousy and the Beetle
Dined, and danced upon their heads
'Til they toddled to their beds.

THE POBBLE WHO HAS NO TOES

EDWARD LEAR

The Pobble who has no toes
Had once as many as we;
When they said "Some day you may lose them all";
He replied "Fish, fiddle-de-dee!"
And his Aunt Jobiska made him drink
Lavender water tinged with pink,
For she said "The World in general knows
There's nothing so good for a Pobble's toes!"

The Pobble who has no toes
Swam across the Bristol Channel;
But before he set out he wrapped his nose
In a piece of scarlet flannel.
For his Aunt Jobiska said "No harm
Can come to his toes if his nose is warm;
And it's perfectly known that a Pobble's toes
Are safe,—provided he minds his nose!"

The Pobble swam fast and well,
And when boats or ships came near him,
He tinkledy-blinkledy-winkled a bell,
So that all the world could hear him.
And all the Sailors and Admirals cried,
When they saw him nearing the further side—
"He has gone to fish for his Aunt Jobiska's
Runcible Cat with crimson whiskers!"

But before he touched the shore,
The shore of the Bristol Channel,
A sea-green porpoise carried away
His wrapper of scarlet flannel.
And when he came to observe his feet,
Formerly garnished with toes so neat,
His face at once became forlorn,
On perceiving that all his toes were gone!

And nobody ever knew,
From that dark day to the present,
Whoso had taken the Pobble's toes,
In a manner so far from pleasant.
Whether the shrimps, or crawfish gray,
Or crafty Mermaids stole them away—
Nobody knew: and nobody knows
How the Pobble was robbed of his twice five toes!

The Pobble who has no toes
Was placed in a friendly Bark,
And they rowed him back, and carried him up
To his Aunt Jobiska's Park.
And she made him a feast at his earnest wish
Of eggs and buttercups fried with fish,—
And she said "It's a fact the whole world knows,
That Pobbles are happier without their toes!"

THE WALRUS AND THE CARPENTER

LEWIS CARROLL

The sun was shining on the sea,
Shining with all his might:
He did his very best to make
The billows smooth and bright—
And this was odd, because it was
The middle of the night.

The moon was shining sulkily,
Because she thought the sun
Had got no business to be there
After the day was done—
"It's very rude of him," she said,
"To come and spoil the fun!"

The sea was wet as wet could be,
The sands were dry as dry.
You could not see a cloud, because
No cloud was in the sky:
No birds were flying overhead—
There were no birds to fly.

The Walrus and the Carpenter
Were walking close at hand:
They wept like anything to see
Such quantities of sand:
"If this were only cleared away,"
They said, "it would be grand."

"If seven maids with seven mops
Swept it for half a year,
Do you suppose," the Walrus said,
"That they could get it clear?"
"I doubt it," said the Carpenter,
And shed a bitter tear.

"O Oysters, come and walk with us!"
  The Walrus did beseech.
"A pleasant walk, a pleasant talk,
  Along the briny beach:
  We cannot do with more than four,
  To give a hand to each."

The eldest Oyster looked at him,
  But never a word he said:
The eldest Oyster winked his eye,
  And shook his heavy head—
Meaning to say he did not choose
  To leave the oyster-bed.

Out four young Oysters hurried up.
  All eager for the treat:
Their coats were brushed, their faces washed,
  Their shoes were clean and neat—
And this was odd, because, you know,
  They hadn't any feet.

Four other Oysters followed them,
  And yet another four;
And thick and fast they came at last,
  And more, and more, and more—
All hopping through the frothy waves,
  And scrambling to the shore.

The Walrus and the Carpenter
  Walked on a mile or so,
And then they rested on a rock
  Conveniently low:
And all the little Oysters stood
  And waited in a row.

"The time has come," the Walrus said,
"To talk of many things:
  Of shoes—and ships—and sealing wax—
  Of cabbages—and kings—
  And why the sea is boiling hot—
  And whether pigs have wings."

"But wait a bit," the Oysters cried,
"Before we have our chat;
  For some of us are out of breath,
  And all of us are fat!"
"No hurry!" said the Carpenter.
  They thanked him much for that.

"A loaf of bread," the Walrus said,
"Is what we chiefly need:
  Pepper and vinegar besides
  Are very good indeed—
  Now, if you're ready, Oysters dear,
  We can begin to feed."

"But not on us!" the Oysters cried,
  Turning a little blue.
"After such kindness, that would be
  A dismal thing to do!"
"The night is fine," the Walrus said,
"Do you admire the view?"

"It was so kind of you to come!
  And you are very nice!"
  The Carpenter said nothing but
"Cut us another slice—
  I wish you were not quite so deaf—
  I've had to ask you twice."

"It seems a shame," the Walrus said:
"I deeply sympathize."
 With sobs and tears he sorted out
 Those of the largest size,
 Holding his pocket-handkerchief
 Before his streaming eyes.

"O Oysters," said the Carpenter,
"You've had a pleasant run!
 Shall we be trotting home again?"
 But answer came there none—
 And this was scarcely odd, because
 They'd eaten every one.

II
My *Home*

May it be delightful my house.
From my head may it be delightful.
To my feet may it be delightful
Where I lie may it be delightful
All above me may it be delightful.
All around me may it be delightful.

—NAVAJO CHANT

O, TO HAVE A LITTLE HOUSE!

THE BABY

GEORGE MACDONALD

Where did you come from, baby dear?
Out of the everywhere into the here.

Where did you get your eyes so blue?
Out of the sky as I came through.

What makes the light in them sparkle and spin?
Some of the starry spikes left in.

Where did you get that little tear?
I found it waiting when I got here.

What makes your forehead so smooth and high?
A soft hand stroked it as I went by.

What makes your cheek like a warm white rose?
Something better than anyone knows.

Whence that three-cornered smile of bliss?
Three angels gave me at once a kiss.

Where did you get that pearly ear?
God spoke, and it came out to hear.

Where did you get those arms and hands?
Love made itself into hooks and bands.

Feet, whence did you come, you darling things?
From the same box as the cherubs' wings.

How did they all just come to be you?
God thought about me, and so I grew.

But how did you come to us, you dear?
God thought of you, and so I am here.

THE BABY'S DANCE
ANN TAYLOR

Dance, little baby, dance up high,
Never mind baby, mother is by;
Crow and caper, caper and crow,
There little baby, there you go:
Up to the ceiling, down to the ground,
Backwards and forwards, round and round.
Then dance, little baby, and mother shall sing,
With the merry gay coral, ding, ding, a-ding, ding.

◎

BABY RUNNING BAREFOOT
D. H. LAWRENCE

When the white feet of the baby beat across the grass
The little white feet nod like white flowers in a wind,
They poise and run like puffs of wind that pass
Over water where the weeds are thinned.

And the sight of their white playing in the grass
Is winsome as a robin's song, so fluttering;
Or like two butterflies that settle on a glass
Cup for a moment, soft little wing-beats uttering.

And I wish that the baby would tack across here to me
Like a wind-shadow running on a pond, so she could stand
With two little bare white feet upon my knee
And I could feel her feet in either hand.

Cool as syringa buds in morning hours,
Or firm and silken as young peony flowers.

LITTLE
DOROTHY ALDIS

I am the sister of him
   And he is my brother.
His is too little for us
   To talk to each other.

So every morning I show him
   My doll and my book;
But every morning he still is
   Too little to look.

○

HIDING
DOROTHY ALDIS

I'm hiding, I'm hiding,
   And no one knows where;
For all they can see is my
   Toes and my hair.

And I just heard my father
   Say to my mother—
"But, darling, he must be
   Somewhere or other;

"Have you looked in the inkwell?"
   And Mother said, "Where?"
"In the *inkwell*," said Father. But
   I was not there.

Then "Wait!" cried my mother—
   "I think that I see
Him under the carpet." But
   It was not me.

"Inside the mirror's
    A pretty good place,"
Said Father and looked, but saw
    Only his face.

"We've hunted," sighed Mother,
    "As hard as we could
And I *am* so afraid that we've
    Lost him for good."

Then I laughed out aloud
    And I wiggled my toes
And Father said—"Look, dear,
    I wonder if those

"Toes could be Benny's?
    There are ten of them, see?"
And they *were* so surprised to find
    Out it was me!

◎

THE WINDOW
WALTER DE LA MARE

Behind the blinds I sit and watch
The people passing—passing by;
And not a single one can see
My tiny watching eye.

◎

MUM IS HAVING A BABY!
COLIN MCNAUGHTON

Mum is having a baby!
    I'm shocked! I'm all at sea!
What's she want another one for:
    WHAT'S THE MATTER WITH ME!?

TO P.J. (2 YRS OLD WHO SED WRITE
A POEM FOR ME IN PORTLAND, OREGON)
SONIA SANCHEZ

if I cud ever write a
poem as beautiful as u
little 2/yr/old/brotha,
I wud laugh, jump, leap
up and touch the stars
cuz u be the poem I try for
each time I pick up a pen and paper.
u. and Morani and Mungu
be our blue/blk/stars that
will shine on our lives and
makes us finally BE.
if I cud ever write a poem as beautiful
as u, little 2/yr/old/brotha,
poetry wud go out of bizness.

◎

A MUSICAL FAMILY
JOHN MOLE

I can play the piano.
I am nearly three.
I can play the long white note
That Mum calls Middle C.

Dad can play the clarinet.
My sister plays the fiddle.
But I'm the one who hits the piano
Slap bang in the middle.

LANGUAGE OF THE BIRDS
JORGE ARQUETA

I used to speak
only Spanish

Now I can speak
English too

And in my dreams
I speak in Nahuatl

the language
my grandma says

her people
—the Pipiles[1]—

learned
from the birds

———

[1]The Pipiles are an indigenous people of El Salvador
  who speak Nahuatl, the language of the Aztecs.

○

FAMILY NEST
JORGE ARQUETA

Today my mama
and my little brothers
arrived from El Salvador

I hardly recognize them
but when we hug each other
we feel like a big nest
with all the birds inside

FOUR GENERATIONS
MARY ANN HOBERMAN

Sometimes when we go out for walks,
I listen while my father talks.

The thing he talks of most of all
Is how it was when he was small

And he went walking with *his* dad
And conversations that they had

About *his* father and the talks
They had when *they* went out for walks.

◎

NEVER DISDAIN DOING THE LEAST GOOD
FROM TEACHINGS OF THE PROPHET MUHAMMAD
AL-BUKHARI

Bukhari..., messenger of Allah, directed me and said,
"Never disdain doing the least good, even greeting your
Brother or sister with a cheerful face."

◎

FROM BROTHER AND SISTER
LEWIS CARROLL

"Sister, sister, go to bed,
  Go and rest your weary head,"
  Thus the prudent brother said.

"Do you want a battered hide
  Or scratches to your face applied?"
  Thus the sister calm replied.

"Sister! do not rouse my wrath,
  I'd make you into mutton broth
  As easily as kill a moth."

The sister raised her beaming eye,
And looked on him indignantly,
And sternly answered "Only try!"

◎

MY HALF

FLORENCE PARRY HEIDE AND ROXANNE HEIDE PIERCE

I share a room
with brother Bob.
We share a bunk bed, too.
Half the room belongs to me,
and half to you-know-who.
Of course it's fair to share a room,
but yet I have the feeling
that since I'm on the upper bunk
my half's just on the ceiling.

◎

TWO IN BED

A. B. ROSS

When my brother Tommy
Sleeps in bed with me,
He doubles up
And makes
himself
exactly
like
a
V
And 'cause the bed is not so wide,
A part of him is on my side.

THE QUARREL

ELEANOR FARJEON

I quarreled with my brother,
I don't know what about,
One thing led to another
And somehow we fell out.
The start of it was slight,
The end of it was strong,
He said he was right,
I knew he was wrong!
We hated one another.
The afternoon turned black.
Then suddenly my brother
Thumped me on the back,
And said, "Oh, *come* along!
We can't go on all night—
I was in the wrong."
So he was in the right.

○

I'M SORRY

MYRA COHN LIVINGSTON

To try to say it,
To put it into words,
To make it come out of my mouth happens slowly.

THERE

I have said it.
Only one small say:
But it is said.

THIS IS JUST TO SAY
WILLIAM CARLOS WILLIAMS

I have eaten
the plums
that were in
the ice box

and which
you were probably
saving
for breakfast

Forgive me
they were delicious
so sweet
and so cold

◦

THINKING TIME
PATRICIA HUBBELL

Our television's broken,
There's silence in the air,
Silence in the living room,
Silence everywhere.

It gives my brain a time to think,
My eyes a time to see—
I love this silent evening time,
Just family and me.

SOMETIMES

MARY ANN HOBERMAN

Sometimes I like to be alone
And look up at the sky
And think my thoughts inside my head—
Just me, myself, and I.

○

SHY

MARY ANN HOBERMAN

Sometimes when I don't want to go
To visit someone I don't know,
They never stop to ask me why.
    She's shy
    They say
    She's shy

Or if we're leaving someone's house,
They say I'm quiet as a mouse
When I forget to say good-bye.
    She's shy
    They say
    She's shy

Cat's got her tongue, they always say,
She often does clam up this way,
She's silent as a stone today.
    She's shy
    They say
    She's shy

I am not shy—or if I am
I'm not a mouse or stone or clam.
I like to look and listen to
What other people say and do.
If I can't think of things to say,
Why should I say things anyway?
I don't see why
That makes me shy

○

THERE WAS A LITTLE GIRL
HENRY WADSWORTH LONGFELLOW

There was a little girl
Who had a little curl
Right in the middle of her forehead.
When she was good
She was very, very good
But when she was bad she was horrid.

○

SHE WAS A PRETTY LITTLE GIRL
RAMÓN PÉREZ DE AYALA
TRANSLATED BY ALIDA MALKUS

She was a pretty little girl.
They spoke to her with all tenderness,
And gave her sweet caresses.

This little girl had a doll.
The doll was very fair
and her name, without question, was Cordelia.

Once upon a time, this is how it was.

The doll, of course, did not speak.
She said nothing to the little girl.
"Why do you not talk like everyone else,
and say tender words to me?"
The little girl asked the doll.
The doll answered not a word.

The little girl, angry, flew into a temper.
She threw the doll upon the floor
and she stamped on it, and broke it.

And then, by a miracle, before she died,
the doll spoke:
"I loved you more than anyone,
but I was not able to tell it."

Once upon a time, this is how it was.

◎

THE LITTLE DOLL

CHARLES KINGSLEY

I once had a sweet little doll, dears,
    The prettiest doll in the world;
Her cheeks were so red and so white, dears,
    And her hair was so charmingly curled.

But I lost my poor little doll, dears,
    As I played in the heath one day;
And I cried for her more than a week, dears;
    But I never could find where she lay.

I found my poor little doll, dears,
    As I played in the heath one day;
Folks say she is terribly changed, dears,
    For her paint is all washed away,

And her arm trodden off by the cows, dears,
    And her hair not the least bit curled:
Yet for old sakes' sake she is still, dears,
    The prettiest doll in the world.

                ◎

TO-DAY'S YOUR NATAL DAY
CHRISTINA GEORGINA ROSSETTI

To-day's your natal day;
    Sweet flowers I bring:
Mother, accept I pray
    My offering.

And may you happy live,
    And long us bless;
Receiving as you give
    Great happiness.

                ◎

FROM SETTING THE TABLE
DOROTHY ALDIS

Evenings
When the house is quiet
I delight
To spread the white
Smooth cloth and put the flowers on the table.

I place the knives and forks around
Without a sound.
I light the candles.

SHABBAT TIME

SYLVIA ROUSS

Soon Shabbat will be here.
A holiday we hold so dear.
Help me set the table now.
Come along, I'll show you how.
The candles have a special place.
On our tablecloth of lace.
Here I place the Kiddush cup.
I take some wine and fill it up.
The challah I shall place right here.
The time for Shabbat is so near.

○

A GRACE FOR A CHILD

ROBERT HERRICK

Here a little child I stand,
Heaving up my either hand,
Cold as paddocks[1] though they be,
Here I lift them up to Thee,
For a benison to fall
On our meat and on us all.

[1]Paddock is an archaic English word for toad.

○

JOHNNY APPLESEED'S BLESSING

O, the Lord is good to me,
And so I thank the Lord
For giving me the things I need,
The sun and the rain and the apple seed.
The Lord is good to me.

A CHILD'S GRACE
ROBERT BURNS

Some hae meat and canna eat,
  And some wad eat that want it;
But we hae meat and we can eat,
  And sae the Lord be thankit.

      ◎

WHOLE DUTY OF CHILDREN
ROBERT LOUIS STEVENSON

A child should always say what's true,
And speak when he is spoken to,
And behave mannerly at table:
At least as far as he is able.

      ◎

A WEAK POEM
(TO BE READ LYING DOWN)
ROGER MCGOUGH

Oh dear, this poem is very weak
It can hardly stand up straight
Which comes from eating junk food
And going to bed too late.

The Cupboard

WALTER DE LA MARE

I know a little cupboard,
With a teeny tiny key,
And there's a jar of Lollipops
    For me, me, me.

It has a little shelf, my dear,
As dark as dark can be,
And there's a dish of Banbury Cakes
    For me, me, me.

I have a small fat grandmamma,
With a very slippery knee,
And she's the Keeper of the Cupboard,
    With the key, key, key.

And when I'm very good, my dear,
As good as good can be,
There's Banbury Cakes, and Lollipops
    For me, me, me.

         ◎

Greedy Jane

"Pudding *and* pie,"
  Said Jane; "O my!"
"Which would you rather?"
  Said her father.
"Both," cried Jane,
  Quite bold and plain.

AFTERNOON WITH GRANDMOTHER

BARBARA A. HUFF

I always shout when Grandma comes,
But Mother says, "Now please be still
And good and do what *Grandma* wants."
And I say, "Yes, I will."

So off we go in Grandma's car.
"There's a brand new movie quite near by,"
She says, "that I'd rather like to see."
And I say, "So would I."

The show has horses and chases and battles;
We gasp and hold hands the whole way through.
She smiles and says, "I liked that lots."
And I say, "I did, too."

"It's made me hungry, though," she says,
"I'd like a malt and tarts with jam.
By any chance are you hungry, too?"
And I say, "Yes, I am."

Later at home my Mother says,
"I hope you were careful to do as bid.
Did you and Grandma have a good time?"
And I say, "YES, WE DID!!!"

SOUL FOOD
CAROLE BOSTON WEATHERFORD

Black-eyed peas, collard greens,
dirty rice and pinto beans,
brown sugar glaze on smokehouse ham,
pickled beets and candied yams;
chicken and dumplings, turkey and stuffin',
buttermilk biscuits and corn bread muffins.
Grandma rose early to prepare this spread,
to bake pound cake and gingerbread,
to shell pecans for Derby pie
and clean a mess of fish to fry.
She asked a blessing before we ate
and always set an extra plate
for an unexpected visitor.
Her home, like her heart, an open door.

○

CHOOSING SHOES
FRIDA WOLFE

New shoes, new shoes,
Red and pink and blue shoes.
Tell me, what would you choose,
If they'd let us buy?

Buckle shoes, bow shoes,
Pretty pointy-toe shoes,
Strappy, cappy low shoes;
Let's have some to try.

Bright shoes, white shoes,
Dandy-dance-by-night shoes,
Perhaps-a-little-tight shoes,
Like some? So would I.

BUT
Flat shoes, fat shoes,
Stump-along-like-that shoes,
Wipe-them-on-the-mat shoes,
That's the sort they'll buy.

◦

MR. NOBODY
I know a funny little man,
    As quiet as a mouse,
Who does the mischief that is done
    In everybody's house!
There's no one ever sees his face,
    And yet we all agree
That every plate we break was cracked
    By Mr. Nobody.

'Tis he who always tears our books,
    Who leaves the door ajar,
He pulls the buttons from our shirts,
    And scatters pins afar;
That squeaking door will always squeak,
    For, prithee, don't you see,
We leave the oiling to be done
    By Mr. Nobody.

The finger marks upon the door
    By none of us are made;
We never leave the blinds unclosed,
    To let the curtains fade.
The ink we never spill; the boots
    That lying round you see
Are not our boots—they all belong
    To Mr. Nobody.

DADDY FELL INTO THE POND

ALFRED NOYES

Everyone grumbled. The sky was gray.
We had nothing to do and nothing to say.
We were nearing the end of a dismal day,
And there seemed to be nothing beyond,
                    THEN
          Daddy fell into the pond!

And everyone's face grew merry and bright,
And Timothy danced for sheer delight.
"Give me the camera, quick, oh quick!
He's crawling out of the duckweed."
Click!

Then the gardener suddenly slapped his knee,
And doubled up, shaking silently,
And the ducks all quacked as if they were daft
And it sounded as if the old drake laughed.

O, there wasn't a thing that didn't respond
                    WHEN
          Daddy fell into the pond!

WHEN YOUNG MELISSA SWEEPS

NANCY BYRD TURNER

When young Melissa sweeps a room
I vow she dances with the broom!

She curtsies in a corner brightly
And leads her partner forth politely.

Then up and down in jigs and reels,
With gold dust flying at their heels,

They caper. With a whirl or two
They make the wainscot shine like new;

They waltz beside the hearth, and quick
It brightens, shabby brick by brick.

A gay gavotte across the floor,
A Highland fling from door to door,

And every crack and corner's clean
Enough to suit a dainty queen.

If ever you are full of gloom,
Just watch Melissa sweep a room!

LITTLE ORPHANT ANNIE

JAMES WHITCOMB RILEY

Little Orphant Annie's come to our house to stay,
An' wash the cups and saucers up, an' brush the crumbs away,
An' shoo the chickens off the porch, an' dust the hearth, an' sweep,
An' make the fire, an' bake the bread, an' earn her board-an'-keep;
An' all us other children, when the supper things is done,
We set around the kitchen fire an' has the mostest fun
A-list'nin' to the witch tales 'at Annie tells about,
An' the Gobble-uns 'at git you
                        Ef you
                    Don't
                        Watch
                        Out!

Onc't they was a little boy wouldn't say his prayers,—
So when he went to bed at night, away upstairs,
His Mammy heerd him holler, an' his Daddy heerd him bawl,
An' when they turn't the kivvers down, he wasn't there at all!
An' they seeked him in the rafter room, an' cubbyhole, an' press,
An' seeked him up the chimbly flue, an' ever'wheres, I guess;
But all they ever found was thist his pants an' roundabout:—
An' the Gobble-uns 'll git you
                        Ef you
                    Don't
                        Watch
                        Out!

An' one time a little girl 'ud allus laugh an' grin,
An' make fun of ever'one, an' all her blood an' kin;
An' onc't, when they was "company," an' ole folks was there,
She mocked 'em an' shocked 'em, an' said she didn't care!
An' thist as she kicked her heels, an' turn't to run an' hide,
They was two great big Black Things a-standin' by her side,
An' they snatched her through the ceilin' 'fore she knowed what
    she's about!
An' the Gobble-uns 'll git you
                    Ef you
                Don't
                    Watch
                    Out!

An' little Orphant Annie says, when the blaze is blue,
An' the lamp-wick sputters, an' the wind goes woo-oo!
An' you hear the crickets quit, an' the moon is gray,
An' the lightnin' bugs in dew is all squenched away,—
You better mind yer parents, and yer teachers fond an' dear,
An' churish them 'at loves you, an' dry the orphant's tear,
An' he'p the pore an' needy ones 'at clusters all about,
Er the Gobble-uns 'll git you
                    Ef you
                Don't
                    Watch
                    Out!

THERE'S SNOW ON THE FIELDS
CHRISTINA GEORGINA ROSSETTI

There's snow on the fields,
  And cold in the cottage,
While I sit in the chimney nook
  Supping hot pottage.

My clothes are soft and warm,
  Fold upon fold,
But I'm so sorry for the poor
  Out in the cold.

○

BREAD AND MILK FOR BREAKFAST
CHRISTINA GEORGINA ROSSETTI

Bread and milk for breakfast,
  And woolen frocks to wear,
And a crumb for robin redbreast
  On the cold days of the year.

○

THE OLD WOMAN OF THE ROADS
PADRAIC COLUM

O, to have a little house!
  To own the hearth and stool and all!
The heaped-up sods upon the fire,
  The pile of turf against the wall!

To have a clock with weights and chains
  And pendulum swinging up and down!
A dresser filled with shining delph,
  Speckled and white and blue and brown!

I could be busy all the day
  Clearing and sweeping hearth and floor
And fixing on their shelf again
  My white and blue and speckled store!

I could be quiet there at night,
  Beside the fire and by myself,
Sure of a bed; and loth to leave
  The ticking clock and the shining delph!

Oh! but I'm weary of mist and dark,
  And roads where there's never a house or bush,
And tired I am of the bog, and the road,
  And the crying wind and the lonesome hush!

And I am praying to God on high,
  And I am praying Him night and day,
For a little house—a house of my own—
  Out of the wind's and the rain's way.

◯

LISTENING

WILLIAM STAFFORD

My father could hear a little animal step,
or a moth in the dark against the screen,
and every far sound called the listening out
into places where the rest of us had never been.

More spoke to him from the soft wild night
than came to our porch for us on the wind;
we would watch him look up and his face go keen
till the walls of the world flared, widened.

My father heard so much that we still stand
inviting the quiet by turning the face,
waiting for a time when something in the night
will touch us too from that other place.

III

Bedtime

In jumping and tumbling
We spend the whole day,
Till night by arriving
Has finished our play.

—ANONYMOUS

HUSH, LITTLE BABY, DON'T SAY A WORD

TUMBLING

CIRCA 1756

In jumping and tumbling
    We spend the whole day,
Till night by arriving
    Has finished our play.

What then? One and all,
    There's no more to be said,
As we tumbled all day,
    So we tumble to bed.

○

BED IN SUMMER

ROBERT LOUIS STEVENSON

In winter I get up at night
And dress by yellow candle-light.
In summer quite the other way,
I have to go to bed by day.

I have to go to bed and see
The birds still hopping on the tree,
Or hear the grown-up people's feet
Still going past me in the street.

And does it not seem hard to you,
When all the sky is clear and blue,
And I should like so much to play,
To have to go to bed by day?

THE MAN IN THE MOON

The man in the moon
Looked out of the moon,
Looked out of the moon and said,
"It's time for you children down there on the earth
To think about getting to bed!"

◎

FROM WEE WILLIE WINKIE
OLD SCOTTISH NURSERY RHYME

Wee Willie Winkie runs through the town,
Upstairs and downstairs in his nightgown,
Peeping through the window, crying through the lock,
"Are all the children in their beds?
For now it's eight o'clock!"

◎

A GOOD BOY
ROBERT LOUIS STEVENSON

I woke before the morning, I was happy all the day,
I never said an ugly word, but smiled and stuck to play.

And now at last the sun is going down behind the wood,
And I am very happy, for I know that I've been good.

My bed is waiting cool and fresh, with linen smooth and fair,
And I must be off to sleepsin-by, and not forget my prayer.

I know that, till to-morrow when I see the sun arise,
No ugly dream shall fright my mind, no ugly sight my eyes.

But slumber hold me tightly till I waken in the dawn,
And hear the thrushes singing in the lilacs round the lawn.

COVERS

NIKKI GIOVANNI

Glass covers windows
to keep the cold away

Clouds cover the sky
to make a rainy day

Nighttime covers
all the things that creep

Blankets cover me
when I'm asleep

○

THE PLUMPUPPETS

CHRISTOPHER MORLEY

When little heads weary have gone to their bed,
When all the good nights and the prayers have been said,
Of all the good fairies that send bairns to rest
The little Plumpuppets are those I love best.

If your pillow is lumpy, or hot, thin, and flat,
The little Plumpuppets know just what they're at:
They plump up the pillow, all soft, cool, and fat—
The little Plumpuppets plump-up it!

The little Plumpuppets are fairies of beds;
They have nothing to do but to watch sleepyheads;
They turn down the sheets and they tuck you in tight,
And they dance on your pillow to wish you good night!

No matter what troubles have bothered the day
Though your doll broke her arm or the pup ran away;
Though your handies are black with the ink that was spilt—
Plumpuppets are waiting in blanket and quilt.

If your pillow is lumpy, or hot, thin, and flat,
The little Plumpuppets know just what they're at:
They plump up the pillow, all soft, cool, and fat—
  The little Plumpuppets plump-up it!

◎

SLEEP, MY CHILD, AND PEACE ATTEND THEE
OLD WELSH LULLABY

Sleep, my child, and peace attend thee,
All through the night,
Guardian angels God will send thee,
All through the night,
Soft the drowsing hours are creeping,
Hill and dale in slumber steeping—
I my loving vigil keeping,
All through the night.

While the moon her watch is keeping,
All through the night,
While the weary world is sleeping,
All through the night,
O'er thy spirit gently stealing
Breathes a pure and holy feeling
While my baby lies a-dreaming,
All through the night.

Love, to thee, my thoughts are turning,
All through the night.
All for thee my heart is yearning,
All through the night.
Though sad fate our lives may sever,
Parting will not last forever—
There's a hope that leaves us never,
All through the night.

WATER NIGHT

OCTAVIO PAZ
TRANSLATED BY MURIEL RUKEYSER

Night with the eyes of a horse that trembles
                  in the night,
night with eyes of water in the field asleep,
is in your eyes, a horse that trembles,
is in your eyes of secret water.

Eyes of shadow-water,
eyes of well-water,
eyes of dream-water.

Silence and solitude,
two little animals moon-led,
drink in your eyes,
drink in those waters.

If you open your eyes,
night opens, doors of musk,
the secret kingdom of the water opens
flowing from the center of the night.

And if you close your eyes,
a river fills you from within,
flows forward, darkens you:
night brings its wetness to beaches in your soul.

○

SEAL LULLABY

RUDYARD KIPLING

Oh! hush thee, my baby, the night is behind us
   And black are the waters that sparkled so green.
The moon, o'er the combers, looks downward to find us
   At rest in the hollows that rustle between.

Where billow meets billow, there soft be thy pillow;
    Ah, weary wee flipperling, curl at thy ease!
The storm shall not wake thee, nor shark overtake thee
    Asleep in the storm of slow-swinging seas.

             ◯

CLOSE NOW THINE EYES AND REST SECURE
FRANCIS QUARLES

Close now thine eyes and rest secure;
Thy soul is safe enough, thy body sure;
He that loves thee, He that keeps
And guards thee, never slumbers, never sleeps.
The smiling conscience in a sleeping breast
Has only peace, has only rest;
The music and the mirth of kings
Are all but very discords, when she sings;
Then close thine eyes and rest secure;
No sleep so sweet as thine, no rest so sure.

             ◯

HUSH, LITTLE BABY, DON'T SAY A WORD
TRADITIONAL LULLABY

Hush, little baby, don't say a word,
Papa's gonna buy you a mockin'bird.

If that mockin'bird won't sing,
Papa's gonna buy you a diamond ring.

If that diamond ring turns brass,
Papa's gonna buy you a lookin' glass.

If that lookin' glass gits broke,
Papa's gonna buy you a horse and yoke.

If that horse and yoke fall over,
Papa's gonna buy you a dog named Rover.

And if that dog named Rover won't bark,
Papa's gonna buy you a goat and cart.

If that goat and cart don't pull,
Papa's gonna buy you a baby bull.

And if that baby bull falls down,
You're still the cutest little baby in town.

WYNKEN, BLYNKEN, AND NOD
EUGENE FIELD

Wynken, Blynken, and Nod one night
Sailed off in a wooden shoe,—
Sailed on a river of crystal light
Into a sea of dew.
"Where are you going, and what do you wish?"
The old moon asked the three.
"We have come to fish for the herring-fish
That live in this beautiful sea;
Nets of silver and gold have we,"
Said Wynken,
Blynken,
And Nod.

The old moon laughed and sang a song,
As they rocked in the wooden shoe;
And the wind that sped them all night long
Ruffled the waves of dew;
The little stars were the herring-fish
That lived in the beautiful sea.
"Now cast your nets wherever you wish,—
Never afraid are we!"
So cried the stars to the fishermen three,
Wynken,
Blynken,
And Nod.

All night long their nets they threw
To the stars in the twinkling foam,—
Then down from the skies came the wooden shoe,
Bringing the fishermen home:
'Twas all so pretty a sail, it seemed
As if it could not be;
And some folk thought 'twas a dream they'd dreamed
Of sailing that beautiful sea;
But I shall name you the fishermen three:
Wynken,
Blynken,
And Nod.

Wynken and Blynken are two little eyes,
And Nod is a little head,
And the wooden shoe that sailed the skies
Is a wee one's trundle-bed;
So shut your eyes while Mother sings
Of wonderful sights that be,
And you shall see the beautiful things
As you rock in the misty sea
Where the old shoe rocked the fishermen three:
Wynken,
Blynken,
And Nod.

○

DREAM
JORGE ARGUETA

Daddy Daddy know what?
Last night I saw a movie
In my pillow

ARITHMETIC IS WHERE YOU HAVE TO MULTIPLY

IV
Friends &
School

The Brain—is wider than the Sky
—*EMILY DICKINSON*

THE CABALIST*

ANGELINA MUÑIZ-HUBERMAN
TRANSLATED BY CHRISTINE DEUTSCH

Abraham, the Cabalist, sat the children down around him
in a circle of light.

He taught them to draw letters.

"The first of them is A; any letter can be made from its lines, and
its sound encompasses every bit of music. If you learn to draw the
letter A, you will possess all the world's secrets."

This is what Abraham, the Cabalist, told the children seated in a
circle of light under Creation's tree of knowledge.

---

*A Cabalist is someone skilled in the mysterious arts.

◎

BEGINNING MY STUDIES

FROM LEAVES OF GRASS
WALT WHITMAN

Beginning my studies the first step pleas'd me so much,
The mere fact consciousness, these forms, the power of motion,
The least insect or animal, the senses, eyesight, love,
The first step I say awed me and pleas'd me so much,
I have hardly gone and hardly wish'd to go any farther,
But stop and loiter all the time to sing it in ecstatic songs.

◎

THE BRAIN IS WIDER THAN THE SKY

The Brain—is wider than the Sky—
    For—put them side by side—
The one the other will include
    With ease—and You—beside—

The Brain is deeper than the sea—
   For—hold them—Blue to Blue—
The one the other will absorb—
   As Sponges, —Buckets—do—.

The Brain is just the weight of God—
   For—Heft them—Pound for Pound—
And they will differ—if they do—
   As Syllable from Sound—

◎

I KEEP SIX HONEST SERVING MEN
FROM THE EPIGRAPH TO "THE ELEPHANT'S CHILD"
RUDYARD KIPLING

I keep six honest serving men
   (They taught me all I knew);
Their names are What and Why and When
And How and Where and Who.

◎

I MEANT TO DO MY WORK TODAY
RICHARD LE GALLIENNE

I meant to do my work today—
But a brown bird sang in the apple tree,
And a butterfly flitted across the field,
And all the leaves were calling me.

And the wind went sighing over the land
Tossing the grasses to and fro,
And a rainbow held out its shining hand—
So what could I do but laugh and go?

FROM THE BAREFOOT BOY
JOHN GREENLEAF WHITTIER

Blessings on thee, little man,
Barefoot boy, with cheek of tan!
With thy turned-up pantaloons,
And thy merry whistled tunes;
With thy red lips, redder still
Kissed by strawberries on the hill;
With the sunshine on thy face,
Through thy torn brim's jaunty grace;
From my heart I give thee joy,—
I was once a barefoot boy!

○

THE SEA BOY
WALTER DE LA MARE

Peter went—and nobody there—
Down by the sandy sea.
And he danced a jig while the moon shone big
All in his lone danced he;
And the surf splashed over his tippeting toes
And he sang his riddle-cum-ree,
With hair a-dangling
Moon a-spangling
The bubbles and froth of the sea.
He danced him to and he danced him fro.
And he twirled himself about,
And now the starry waves tossed in,
And now the waves washed out;
Bare as an acorn, bare as a nut,
Nose and toes and knee,
Peter the sea-boy danced and pranced,
And sang his riddle-cum-ree.

Often I think of the beautiful town

FROM EVANGELINE: A TALE OF ACADIE
HENRY WADSWORTH LONGFELLOW

Often I think of the beautiful town
   That is seated by the sea;
Often in thought go up and down
The pleasant streets of that dear old town,
   And youth comes back to me.
     And a verse of a Lapland song
     Is haunting my memory still:
     "A boy's will is the wind's will,
And the thoughts of youth are long, long thoughts."

I can see the shadowy lines of its trees,
   And catch, in sudden gleams,
The sheen of the far-surrounding seas,
And islands that were the Hesperides
   Of all my boyish dreams.
     And the burden of that old song,
     It murmurs and whispers still:
     "A boy's will is the wind's will,
And the thoughts of youth are long, long thoughts."

◎

Favorite Book

BARBARA NAFTALI MEYERS

Today, picking up a book
         by its front cover

was like lifting a very small baby
         up by one arm.

THE LIBRARY

BARBARA A. HUFF

It looks like any building
When you pass it on the street,
Made of stone and glass and marble,
Made of iron and concrete.

But once inside you can ride
A camel or a train,
Visit Rome, Siam, or Nome,
Feel a hurricane,
Meet a king, learn to sing,
How to bake a pie,
Go to sea, plant a tree,
Find how airplanes fly,
Train a horse, and of course
Have all the dogs you'd like,
See the moon, a sandy dune,
Or catch a whopping pike.
Everything that books can bring
You'll find inside those walls.
A world is there for you to share
When adventure calls.

You cannot tell its magic
By the way the building looks,
But there's wonderment within it,
The wonderment of books.

Eating Poetry

MARK STRAND

Ink runs from the corners of my mouth.
There is no happiness like mine.
I have been eating poetry.

The librarian does not believe what she sees.
Her eyes are sad
and she walks with her hands in her dress.

The poems are gone.
The light is dim.
The dogs are on the basement stairs and coming up.

Their eyeballs roll,
their blond legs burn like brush.
The poor librarian begins to stamp her feet and weep.

She does not understand.
When I get on my knees and lick her hand,
she screams.

I am a new man.
I snarl at her and bark.
I romp with joy in the bookish dark.

I Love the Look of Words

MAYA ANGELOU

Popcorn leaps, popping from the floor
of a hot black skillet
and into my mouth.
Black words leap,
snapping from the white
page. Rushing into my eyes. Sliding
into my brain which gobbles them
the way my tongue and teeth
chomp the buttered popcorn.

When I have stopped reading,
ideas from the words stay stuck
in my mind, like the sweet
smell of butter perfuming my
fingers long after the popcorn
is finished.

I love the book and the look of words
the weight of ideas that popped into my mind
I love the tracks
of new thinking in my mind.

○

Vocabulary Word

CELESTINE FROST

Peanuts are the favorite—
(Some call them goober peas)
And you may also choose
To chew on these.
But don't *eschew* the cashew,
If you please!

ARITHMETIC

CARL SANDBURG

Arithmetic is where numbers fly like pigeons in and out of your
head.

Arithmetic tells you how many you lose or win if you know how
many you had before you lost or won.

Arithmetic is seven eleven all good children go to heaven—or five
six bundle of sticks.

Arithmetic is numbers you squeeze from your head to your hand to
your pencil to your paper till you get the answer.

Arithmetic is where the answer is right and everything is nice and
you can look out of the window and see the blue sky or the
answer is wrong and you have to start all over and try again and
see how it comes out this time.

If you take a number and double it and double it again and then
double it a few more times, the number gets bigger and bigger
and goes higher and higher and only arithmetic can tell you what
the number is when you decide to quit doubling.

Arithmetic is where you have to multiply—and you carry the
multiplication table in your head and hope you won't lose it.

If you have two animal crackers, one good and one bad, and you eat
one and a striped zebra with streaks all over him eats the other,
how many animal crackers will you have if somebody offers you
five six seven and you say No no no and you say Nay nay nay and
you say Nix nix nix?

If you ask your mother for one fried egg for breakfast and she gives
you two fried eggs and you eat both of them, who is better in
arithmetic, you or your mother?

PENCILS ARE MY FAVORITE THINGS

LOU LAHR

Pencils are my favorite things:
I can draw the bird with wings.

I can draw the bird that flies:

I follow it, follow it with my eyes.

I can draw as he comes back,
the worm a-dangling from his beak.

I can draw his nesting tree,
And clouds above it, floating free.

I can draw the cat that climbs,
Creeping out along the limb,

I can draw the dog that barks,
Alerting the robin that danger stalks.

Pencils are my favorite things:
I can draw most anything.

◎

BROWN

ARTHUR GREEN

Brown is my favorite color,
A many-splendored mud:

There's auburn which is deep and rich
(though not so red as blood);

There're ochres, umbers, ambers,
And there are blacks and blues;

There's purplish and yellow-brown
And other hidden hues.

They make a subtle spectrum—
Those called "beige" are pale;

There's sand and clay, both pink and gray,
And, darkly green, there's marl.

Oh, I could make a rainbow
Out of earth-brown clay

If I had no other paint
With which to play.

Yes, I could paint with mud,
For if I dig deep down

The layers of earth are many-hued
While always being brown.

PAD AND PENCIL
DAVID MCCORD

I drew a rabbit. John erased him
and not the dog I said had chased him.

I drew a bear on another page,
but John said, "Put him in a cage."

I drew some mice. John drew the cat
with nasty claws. The mice saw that.

I got them off the page real fast:
the things I draw don't ever last.

We drew a bird with one big wing:
he couldn't fly worth anything,

but sat there crumpled on a limb.
John's pencil did a job on him.

Three bats were next. I made them fly.
John smudged one out against the sky

above an owl he said could hoot.
He helped me with my wolf. The brute

had lots too long a tail, but we
concealed it all behind a tree.

By then I couldn't think of much
except to draw a rabbit hutch;

but since we had no rabbit now
I drew what must have been a cow,

with curvy horns stuck through the slats—
they both looked something like the bats.

And feeling sad about the bear
inside his cage, I saw just where

I'd draw the door to let him out.
And that's just all of it, about.

○

MY PICTURE
ROBERT SERVICE

I made a picture; all my heart
I put in it, and all I knew
Of canvas-cunning and of Art,
Of tenderness and passion true.
A worshipped Master came to see;
Oh he was kind and gentle, too.
He studied it with sympathy,
And sensed what I had sought to do.

Said he: "Your paint is fresh and fair,
And I can praise it without cease;
And yet a touch just here and there
Would make of it a masterpiece."
He took the brush from out my hand;
He touched it here, he touched it there.
So well he seemed to understand,
And momently it grew more fair.

Oh there was nothing I could say,
And there was nothing I could do.
I thanked him, and he went his way,
And then—I slashed my picture through.
For though his brush with soft caress
Had made my daub a thing divine,
Oh God! I wept with bitterness,
...It wasn't mine, it wasn't mine.

◦

GOOD SPORTSMANSHIP
RICHARD ARMOUR

Good sportsmanship we hail, we sing,
        It's always pleasant when you spot it.
There's only one unhappy thing:
        You have to lose to prove you've got it.

◦

THE RUNNER
WALT WHITMAN

On a flat road runs the well-train'd runner,
He is lean and sinewy with muscular legs,
He is thinly clothed, he leans forward as he runs,
With lightly closed fists and arms partially rais'd.

CRYSTAL ROWE
(TRACK STAR)
MEL GLENN

Allthegirlsarebunched
togetheratthestarting
_____line_____

But

When the gun goes off

I

J

U

M

P

out ahead and

never look back

and

HIT

the

___T___A___P___E___

a

WINNER!

POINT SCORED
CHARLOTTE CARDENAS DWYER

up against the backboard · · · leaning · · · almost in · · · lolling · · · looping

○

ON THE SKATEBOARD
LILLIAN MORRISON

Skimming
an asphalt sea
I swerve, I curve, I
sway; I speed to whirring
sound an inch above the
ground; I'm the sailor
and the sail, I'm the
driver and the wheel
I'm the one and only
single engine
human auto
mobile.

POPSICLE

JOAN BRANSFIELD GRAHAM

Popsicle
Popsicle
t i c k l e
tongue fun
l i c k s i c l e
s t i c k s i c l e
p l e a s e
don't run
d r i p s i c l e
s l i p s i c l e
melt, melt
t r i c k y
s t o p s i c l e
p l o p s i c l e
hand all
s
t
i
c
k
y

SICK

SHEL SILVERSTEIN

"I cannot go to school today,"
 Said little Peggy Ann McKay.
"I have the measles and the mumps,
 A gash, a rash and purple bumps.
 My mouth is wet, my throat is dry,
 I'm going blind in my right eye.
 My tonsils are as big as rocks,
 I've counted sixteen chicken pox
 And there's one more—that's seventeen,
 And don't you think my face looks green?
 My leg is cut—my eyes are blue—
 It might be instamatic flu.
 I cough and sneeze and gasp and choke,
 I'm sure that my left leg is broke—
 My hip hurts when I move my chin,
 My belly button's caving in,
 My back is wrenched, my ankle's sprained,
 My 'pendix pains each time it rains.

 My nose is cold, my toes are numb.
 I have a sliver in my thumb.
 My neck is stiff, my voice is weak,
 I hardly whisper when I speak.
 My tongue is filling up my mouth,
 I think my hair is falling out.
 My elbow's bent, my spine ain't straight,
 My temperature is one-o-eight.
 My brain is shrunk, I cannot hear,
 There is a hole inside my ear.
 I have a hangnail, and my heart is—what?
 What's that? What's that you say?
 You say today is … Saturday?
 G'bye, I'm going out to play!"

NAPOLEON

MIROSLAV HOLUB

Children, when was
Napoleon Bonaparte born,
Asks the teacher.

A thousand years ago, the children say.
A hundred years ago, the children say.
Last year, the children say.
No one knows.

Children, what did
Napoleon Bonaparte do,
asks the teacher.

Won a war, the children say.
Lost a war, the children say.
No one knows.

Our butcher had a dog
called Napoleon,
says Frantisek.
The butcher used to beat him and the dog died
of hunger
a year ago.

And all the children are now sorry
for Napoleon.

LITTLE GIRL, BE CAREFUL WHAT YOU SAY

CARL SANDBURG

Little girl, be careful what you say
when you make talk with words, words—
for words are made of syllables
and syllables, child, are made of air—
and air is so thin—air is the breath of God—
air is finer than fire or mist,
finer than water or moonlight,
finer than spider-webs in the moon,
finer than water-flowers in the morning:
    and words are strong, too,
    stronger than rocks or steel
stronger than potatoes, corn, fish, cattle,
and soft, too, soft as little pigeon-eggs,
soft as the music of hummingbird wings.
    So, little girl, when you speak greetings,
when you tell jokes, make wishes or prayers,
    be careful, be careless, be careful,
    be what you wish to be.

I AM ROSE

GERTRUDE STEIN

I am Rose my eyes are blue
I am Rose and who are you?
I am Rose and when I sing
I am Rose like anything.

Song of the Yeshiva Bocher

AHRON HUEBNER

I saw a child. I said, "My boy."
da tum da tum da tum da tum

I saw my mother. I said, "Hi, my boy."
da tum da tum da tum da tum

I went to school. I saw my rebbi
and said to him, "Hello, my boy."
da tum da tum da tum da tum

He said, "You're going to the principal."
da tum da tum da tum da tum

I saw my principal and said
"How are you, my boy." He said,

"What chutzpa! You're expelled from school."
da tum da tum   da tum da tum

Then I went home. I saw my Dad.
His face was red. Big flames came up
out of his head.
da tum da tum   da tum da tum

To him I said, "I tried to be good,
my boy."

TOMÁS'S LIE
JORGE ARGUETA

Tomás you are
a liar

You told me
that birds fly because
they have engines
in their butts

Liar

Some have engines
in their wings
and others in their beaks

◎

SONG OF MAN CHIPPING AN ARROWHEAD
W. S. MERWIN

Little children you will all go
But the one you are hiding
Will fly

◎

THE ARROW AND THE SONG
HENRY WADSWORTH LONGFELLOW

I shot an arrow into the air,
It fell to earth, I knew not where;
For, so swiftly it flew, the sight
Could not follow it in its flight.

I breathed a song into the air,
It fell to earth, I knew not where;
For who has sight so keen and strong,
That it can follow the flight of song?

Long, long afterward, in an oak
I found the arrow, still unbroke;
And the song, from beginning to end,
I found again in the heart of a friend.

◎

JENNY WHITE AND JOHNNY BLACK
ELEANOR FARJEON

Jenny White and Johnny Black
Went out for a walk.
Jenny found wild strawberries,
And John a lump of chalk.

Jenny White and Johnny Black
Clambered up a hill.
Jenny heard a willow-wren
And John a workman's drill.

Jenny White and Johnny Black
Wandered by the dyke.
Jenny smelt the meadow-sweet,
And John a motor-bike.

Jenny White and Johnny Black
Turned into a lane.
Jenny saw the moon by day
And Johnny saw a train.

Jenny White and Johnny Black
Walked into a storm.
Each felt for the other's hand
And found it nice and warm.

PRIORITIES OF SOME MEXICAN CHILDREN
JIMMY CARTER

A sign was leaning toward adobe shacks
back from the road, across a dry plateau.
LLANOS it read, the same as our Plains.
When we stopped to photograph the view
three black-haired children hurried down a path
shouting something, eager to be heard.
"Get out your pocketbooks," I said,
"I can guess the word."
When they got closer, we could tell
it was not *dinero* but
lápiz and *papel.*

---

lápiz = pencil; *papel* = paper

○

THE RAILWAY CHILDREN
SEAMUS HEANEY

When we climbed the slopes of the cutting
We were eye-level with the white cups
Of the telegraph poles and the sizzling wires.

Like lovely freehand they curved for miles
East and miles west beyond us, sagging
Under their burden of swallows.

We were small and thought we knew nothing
Worth knowing. We thought words traveled the wires
In the shiny pouches of raindrops,

Each one seeded full with the light
Of the sky, the gleam of the lines, and ourselves
So infinitesimally scaled

We could stream through the eye of a needle.

TIMOTHY WINTERS

CHARLES CAUSLEY

Timothy Winters comes to school
With eyes as wide as a football pool,
Ears like bombs and teeth like splinters:
A blitz of a boy is Timothy Winters.

His belly is white, his neck is dark,
And his hair is an exclamation mark.
His clothes are enough to scare a crow
And through his britches the blue winds blow.

When teacher talks he won't hear a word
And he shoots down dead the arithmetic-bird,
He licks the patterns off his plate
And he's not even heard of the Welfare State.

Timothy Winters has bloody feet
And he lives in a house on Suez Street,
He sleeps in a sack on the kitchen floor
And they say there aren't boys like him anymore.

Old Man Winters likes his beer
And his missus ran off with a bombardier,
Grandma sits in the grate with a gin
And Timothy's dosed with an aspirin.

The Welfare Worker lies awake
But the law's as tricky as a ten-foot snake,
So Timothy Winters drinks his cup
And slowly goes on growing up.

At Morning Prayers the Headmaster helves
For children less fortunate than ourselves,
And the loudest response in the room is when
Timothy Winters roars "Amen!"

So come one angel, come on ten:
Timothy Winters says "Amen"
Amen amen amen amen.
Timothy Winters, Lord.

                  Amen.

○

ORPHANAGE

*TO THE ARTIST DENIS RUIZ
BY BARBARA NAFTALI MEYERS*

Left, to the greenish

walls, and nuns' lips
grown thin from love
of God, he knows why

he is there. For sure,
his father is a king
and means to have him

show, that he can take
those blows, unwincing.
So, when his father dies

he'll be prepared, to
follow in his place
grown princely from the

switches in his face.
This morning cook's
eyes seemed so wide, it

hurt his own to look.
Put away where the
others won't see, he

has shining armor.

WHEN THAT I WAS AND A TINY LITTLE BOY

FROM TWELFTH NIGHT, *ACT V, SCENE I*
WILLIAM SHAKESPEARE

When that I was and a tiny little boy,
With a hey, ho, the wind and the rain,
A foolish thing was but a toy,
For the rain it raineth every day.

○

SOMEBODY'S MOTHER

The woman was old, and ragged, and gray,
And bent with the chill of the winter's day;

The street was wet with a recent snow,
And the woman's feet were aged and slow.

She stood at the crossing and waited long,
Alone, uncared for, amid the throng

Of human beings who passed her by,
Nor heeded the glance of her anxious eye.

Down the street, with laughter and shout,
Glad in the freedom of "school let out,"

Came boys like a flock of sheep,
Hailing the snow piled white and deep.

Past the woman so old and gray
Hastened the children on their way,

Nor offered a helping hand to her—
So meek, so timid, afraid to stir

Lest the carriage wheels or the horses' feet
Should crowd her down in the slippery street.

At last came one of the merry troop—
The gayest laddie of all the group;

He paused beside her and whispered low,
"I'll help you across if you wish to go."

Her aged hand on his strong young arm
She placed, and so, without hurt or harm,

He guided the trembling feet along,
Proud that his own were firm and strong.

Then back again to his friends he went,
His young heart happy and well content.

"She's somebody's mother, boys, you know,
For all she's aged and poor and slow;

"And I hope some fellow will lend a hand
To help my mother, you understand,

"If ever she's poor and old and gray,
When her own dear boy is far away."

And "somebody's mother" bowed low her head
In her home that night and the prayer she said

Was, "God be kind to the noble boy
Who is somebody's son and pride and joy!"

FROM There Was a Child Went Forth

FROM LEAVES OF GRASS
WALT WHITMAN

There was a child went forth every day;
And the first object he looked upon, that object he became;
And that object became part of him for the day, or a certain part
    of the day, or for many years, or stretching cycles of years.

The early lilacs became part of this child,
And grass, and white and red morning-glories, and white and red
    clover, and the song of the phoebe-bird,
And the Third-month lambs, and the sow's pink-faint litter, and the
    mare's foal, and the cow's calf,
And the noisy brood of the barnyard or by the mire of the pond-side,
And the fish suspending themselves so curiously below there—and
    the beautiful curious liquid,
And the water-plants with their graceful flat heads—all became
    part of him.

The field-sprouts of Fourth-month and Fifth-month became part of
   him;
Winter-grain sprouts, and those of the light-yellow corn, and the
    esculent roots of the garden,
And the apple-trees cover'd with blossoms, and the fruit afterward,
    and wood-berries, and the commonest weeds by the road;
And the old drunkard staggering home from the out-house of the
    tavern, whence he had lately risen,
And the school-mistress that pass'd on her way to the school,
And the friendly boys that pass'd—and the quarrelsome boys,
And the tidy and fresh-cheek'd girls—and the barefoot Negro boy
    and girl,
And all the changes of city and country, wherever he went.

His own parents,

He that had father'd him, and she that had conceiv'd him in her womb,
   and birth'd him,

They gave this child more of themselves than that;

They gave him afterward every day—they became part of him.

The mother at home, quietly placing the dishes on the supper-table;

The mother with mild words—clean her cap and gown, a
      wholesome odor falling off her person and clothes as she
      walks by;

The father, strong, self-sufficient, manly, mean, anger'd, unjust;

The blow, the quick loud word, the tight bargain, the crafty lure,

The usages, the language, the company, the furniture—the yearning
      and swelling heart,

Affection that will not be gainsay'd—the sense of what is real—the
      thought if, after all, it should prove unreal,

The doubts of day-time and the doubts of night-time—the curious
      whether and how,

Whether that which appears so is so, or is it all flashes and specks?

Men and women crowding fast in the streets—if they are not
      flashes and specks, what are they?

The streets themselves, and the façades of houses, and goods
      in the windows,

Vehicles, teams, the heavy-plank'd wharves—the huge crossing at
      the ferries,

The village on the highland, seen from afar at sunset—the river
      between,

Shadows, aureola and mist, the light falling on roofs and gables of
      white or brown, three miles off,

The schooner near by, sleepily dropping down the tide—the little boat
      slack-tow'd astern,

The hurrying tumbling waves, quick-broken crests, slapping,

The strata of color'd clouds, the long bar of maroon-tint, away
    solitary by itself—the spread of purity it lies motionless in,
The horizon's edge, the flying sea-crow, the fragrance of salt marsh
    and shore mud;
These became part of that child who went forth every day, and who
    now goes, and will always go forth every day.

○

THE THOUSANDTH MAN

RUDYARD KIPLING

One man in a thousand, Solomon says,
Will stick more close than a brother.
And it's worth while seeking him half your days
If you find him before the other.
Nine hundred and ninety-nine depend
On what the world sees in you,
But the Thousandth man will stand your friend
With the whole round world agin you.

'Tis neither promise nor prayer nor show
Will settle the finding for 'ee.
Nine hundred and ninety-nine of 'em go
By your looks, or your acts, or your glory.
But if he finds you and you find him.
The rest of the world don't matter;
For the Thousandth Man will sink or swim
With you in any water.

You can use his purse with no more talk
Than he uses yours for his spendings,
And laugh and meet in your daily walk
As though there had been no lendings.
Nine hundred and ninety-nine of 'em call
For silver and gold in their dealings;
But the Thousandth Man he's worth 'em all,
Because you can show him your feelings.

His wrong's your wrong, and his right's your right,
In season or out of season.
Stand up and back it in all men's sight—
With that for your only reason!
Nine hundred and ninety-nine can't bide
The shame or mocking or laughter,
But the Thousandth Man will stand by your side
To the gallows-foot—and after!

V

Animal
Friends

...and a mouse is miracle enough to
stagger sextillions of infidels

—WALT WHITMAN

O TO BE A DRAGON...AT TIMES INVISIBLE

YOUR CATFISH FRIEND
RICHARD BRAUTIGAN

If I were to live my life
in catfish forms
in scaffolds of skin and whiskers
at the bottom of a pond
and you were to come by
one evening
when the moon was shining
down into my dark home
and stand there at the edge
of my affection
and think, "It's beautiful
here by this pond. I wish
somebody loved me,"
I'd love you and be your catfish
friend and drive such lonely
thoughts from your mind
and suddenly you would be
at peace,
and ask yourself, "I wonder
if there are any catfish
in this pond? It seems like
a perfect place for them."

○

THE TURTLE
WILLIAM CARLOS WILLIAMS
FOR HIS GRANDSON

Not because of his eyes,
      the eyes of a bird,
           but because he is beaked,
birdlike, to do an injury,
      has the turtle attracted you.
           He is your only pet.
When we are together

you talk of nothing else
                ascribing all sorts
of murderous motives
        to his least action.
                You ask me
to write a poem,
        should I have poems to write,
                about a turtle.

The turtle lives in the mud
        but is not mud-like,
                you can tell by his eyes
which are clear.
        When he shall escape
                his present confinement
he will stride about the world
        destroying all
                with his sharp beak.
Whatever opposes him
        in the streets of the city
                shall go down.
Cars will be overturned.
        And upon his back
                shall ride,
to his conquests,
    my Lord,
                you!

You shall be master!
        In the beginning
                there was a great tortoise
who supported the world.
        Upon him
                all ultimately
rests.
        Without him
                nothing will stand.

He is all wise
       and can outrun the hare.
           In the night
his eyes carry him
     to unknown places.
          He is your friend.

○

POEM (AS THE CAT)
WILLIAM CARLOS WILLIAMS

As the cat
climbed over
the top of

the jamcloset
first the right
forefoot

carefully
then the hind
stepped down

into the pit of
the empty
flower pot

○

COYOTE
WILLIAM STAFFORD

My left hind-
foot
    steps
in the track of my right
fore-
    foot

and my hind-right
foot
          steps
in the track of my
fore-left
          foot
and so on, for miles—

Me paying no attention, while
my nose rides along letting
the full report, the
whole blast of the countryside
come along toward me
on rollers of scent, and—

I come home with a chicken or
a rabbit and sit up
singing all night with my friends.
It's baroque, my life, and
I tell it on the mountain.

I wouldn't trade it for yours.

○

O WILD GOOSE

ISSA
TRANSLATED FROM THE JAPANESE BY MATTHEW GOLUB

O wild goose,
     How young were you
     When you set out alone?

THE LITTLE BLACK DOG
MARGARET WISE BROWN

I had a little black dog
And the sun came out for him
And it shone on his curious little nose
And warmed him warm under his black fur
And he bounded through his sunlight
The sunlight that shone for him.

○

BABY FIREFLY
ISSA
TRANSLATED FROM THE JAPANESE BY MATTHEW GOLUB

Baby firefly—
    Do my hand's wrinkles
    Make it hard to walk?

○

LITTLE TALK
AILEEN FISHER

Don't you think it's probable
that beetles, bugs, and bees
talk about a lot of things—
you know, such things as these:

The kind of weather where they live
in jungles tall with grass
and earthquakes in their villages
whenever people pass!

Of course, we'll never know if bugs
talk very much at all,
because our ears are far too big
for talk that is so small.

Please, don't swat!

ISSA
TRANSLATED FROM THE JAPANESE BY MATTHEW GOLUB

Please, don't swat!
        the housefly begs,
        rubbing its hands and feet.

○

Archy, the Cockroach, Speaks

FROM "CERTAIN MAXIMS OF ARCHY"
DON MARQUIS

i heard a
couple of fleas
talking the other
days says one come
to lunch with
me I can lead you
to a pedigreed
dog says the
other one
I do not care
what a dog s
pedigree may be
safety first
is my motto what
I want to know
is whether he
has got a
muzzle on
millionaires and
bums taste
about alike to me

A SILENT TOAD

ISSA
TRANSLATED FROM THE JAPANESE BY MATTHEW GOLUB

A silent toad—
   the face of one
      bursting with much to say

◎

LIZARDS

ALEXIS GONZÁLEZ

Behind my grandfather's house
  There is a hill
    Where I catch baby lizards.
I let them bite my ears
  So I can wear them
    Like earrings.

◎

THE WORM

RALPH BERGENGREN

When the earth is turned in spring
The worms are fat as anything.

And birds come flying all around
To eat the worms right off the ground.

They like worms just as much as I
Like bread and milk and apple pie.

And once, when I was very young,
I put a worm right on my tongue.

I didn't like the taste a bit,
And so I didn't swallow it.

But oh, it makes my Mother squirm
Because she *thinks* I ate that worm!

ALL BUT BLIND
WALTER DE LA MARE

All but blind
    In his chambered hole
Gropes for worms
    The four-clawed Mole.

All but blind
    In the evening sky,
The hooded Bat
    Twirls softly by.

All but blind
    In the burning day
The Barn-Owl blunders
    On her way.

And blind as are
    These three to me,
So, blind to Some-one
    I must be.

THE CITY MOUSE LIVES IN A HOUSE
CHRISTINA GEORGINA ROSSETTI

The city mouse lives in a house;—
    The garden mouse lives in a bower.
He's friendly with the frogs and toads
    And sees the pretty plants in flower.

The city mouse eats bread and cheese;—
    The garden mouse eats what he can;
We will not grudge him seeds and stalks,
    Poor little timid furry man.

THE MOUSE

ELIZABETH COATSWORTH

I heard a mouse
Bitterly complaining
In a crack of moonlight
Aslant on the floor—

"Little I ask
And that little is not granted.
There are few crumbs
In this world any more.

"The bread-box is tin
And I cannot get in.

"The jam's in a jar
My teeth cannot mar.

"The cheese sits by itself
On the pantry shelf—

"All night I run
Searching and seeking,
All night I run
About on the floor.

"Moonlight is there
And a bare place for dancing,
But no little feast
Is spread any more."

○

WHAT BECAME OF THEM?

He was a rat, and she was a rat,
    And down in one hole they did dwell;
And both were as black as a witch's cat,
    And they loved one another well.

He had a tail, and she had a tail,
    Both long and curling and fine;
And each said, 'Yours is the finest tail
    In the world, excepting mine.'

He smelt the cheese, and she smelt the cheese,
    And they both pronounced it good;
And both remarked it would greatly add
    To the charms of their daily food.

So he ventured out, and she ventured out,
    And I saw them go with pain;
But what befell them I never can tell,
    For they never came back again.

○

THE MYSTERIOUS CAT
VACHEL LINDSAY

I saw a proud, mysterious cat,
I saw a proud, mysterious cat,
Too proud to catch a mouse or rat—
        Mew, mew, mew.
But catnip she would eat, and purr,
But catnip she would eat, and purr.
And goldfish she did much prefer—
        Mew, mew, mew.
I saw a cat—'twas but a dream,
I saw a cat—'twas but a dream,
Who scorned the slave that brought her cream—
        Mew, mew, mew.
Unless the slave were dressed in style,
Unless the slave were dressed in style,
And knelt before her all the while—
        Mew, mew, mew.

Did you ever hear of a thing like that?

Did you ever hear of a thing like that?
Did you ever hear of a thing like that?
Oh, what a proud, mysterious cat.
Oh, what a proud, mysterious cat.
Oh, what a proud, mysterious cat.
     Mew ... mew ... mew.

○

A BIRD CAME DOWN THE WALK
EMILY DICKINSON

A Bird came down the Walk—
He did not know I saw—
He bit an Angleworm in halves
And ate the fellow, raw,

And then he drank a Dew
from a convenient Grass—
And then hopped sidewise to the Wall
To let a Beetle pass—

He glanced with rapid eyes
That hurried all around—
They looked like frightened Beads, I thought—
He stirred his Velvet Head

Like one in danger, Cautious,
I offered him a Crumb
And he unrolled his feathers
And rowed him softer home—

Than Oars divide the Ocean,
Too silver for a seam—
Or Butterflies, off Banks of Noon
Leap, plashless as they swim.

A NARROW FELLOW IN THE GRASS

EMILY DICKINSON

A narrow Fellow in the Grass
Occasionally rides—
You may have met Him—did you not
His notice sudden is—

The Grass divides as with a Comb—
A spotted shaft is seen—
And then it closes at your feet
And opens further on—

He likes a Boggy Acre
A Floor too cool for Corn—
Yet when a Boy, and Barefoot—
I more than once at Noon
Have passed, I thought, a Whip lash
Unbraiding in the Sun
When stooping to secure it
It wrinkled, and was gone—

Several of Nature's People
I know, and they know me—
I feel for them a transport
Of cordiality—

But never met this Fellow
Attended, or alone
Without a tighter breathing
And Zero at the Bone—

THE SKUNK

ROBERT P. TRISTRAM COFFIN

When the sun has slipped away
And the dew is on the day,
Then the creature comes to call
Men malign the most of all.

The little skunk is very neat,
With his sensitive, plush feet
And a dainty, slim head set
With diamonds on bands of jet.

He walks upon his evening's duty
Of declaring how that beauty
With her patterns is not done
At the setting of the sun.

He undulates across the lawn,
He asks nobody to fawn
On his graces. All that he
Asks is that men let him be.

He knows that he is very fine
In every clean and rippling line,
He is a conscious black and white
Little symphony of night.

○

THE WOLF CRY

LEW SARETT

The Arctic moon hangs overhead;
The wide white silence lies below.
A starveling pine stands lone and gaunt,
Black-penciled on the snow.

Weird as the moan of sobbing winds,
A lone long call floats up from the trail;
And the naked soul of the frozen North
Trembles in that wail.

◎

THE UNKNOWN COLOR
COUNTEE CULLEN

I've often heard my mother say,
When great winds blew across the day,
And, cuddled close and out of sight,
The young pigs squealed with sudden fright
Like something speared or javelined,
"Poor little pigs, they see the wind."

◎

THE NORTH WIND DOTH BLOW

The north wind doth blow
And we shall have snow,
And what will poor robin do then?
Poor thing.

He'll sit in the barn
To keep himself warm,
And hide his head under his wing,
Poor thing.

◎

FOUR LITTLE FOXES
LEW SARETT

Speak gently, Spring, and make no sudden sound;
For in my windy valley, yesterday I found
New-born foxes squirming on the ground—
        Speak gently.

Walk gently, March; forbear the bitter blow;
Her feet within a trap, her blood upon the snow,
The four little foxes saw their mother go—
        Walk softly.

Go lightly, Spring; oh, give them no alarm;
When I covered them with boughs to shelter them from harm,
The thin blue foxes suckled at my arm—
        Go lightly.

Step softly, March, with your rampant hurricane;
Nuzzling one another, and whimpering with pain,
The new little foxes are shivering in the rain—
        Step softly.

FROM THE SHORE

CARL SANDBURG

A lone gray bird,
Dim-dipping, far-flying,
Alone in the shadows and grandeurs and tumults
Of night and the sea
And the stars and storms.

Out over the darkness it wavers and hovers,
Out into the gloom it swings and batters,
Out into the wind and the rain and the vast,
Out into the pit of a great black world,
Where fogs are at battle, sky-driven, sea-blown,
Love of mist and rapture of flight,
Glories of chance and hazards of death
On its eager and palpitant wings.

Out into the deep of the great dark world,
Beyond the long borders where foam and drift
Of the sundering waves are lost and gone
On the tides that plunge and rear and crumble.

SYMPATHY

PAUL LAURENCE DUNBAR

I know what the caged bird feels, alas!
When the sun is bright on the upland slopes;
When the wind stirs soft through the springing grass,
And the river flows like a stream of glass;
When the first bird sings and the first bud opes,
And the faint perfume from its chalice steals—
I know what the caged bird feels!

I know why the caged bird beats his wing
Till its blood is red on the cruel bars;
For he must fly back to his perch and cling
When he fain would be on the bough a-swing;
And a pain still throbs in the old, old scars
And they pulse again with a keener sting—
I know why he beats his wing!

I know why the caged bird sings, ah me,
When his wing is bruised and his bosom sore,—
When he beats his bars and he would be free;
It is not a carol of joy or glee,
But a prayer that he sends from his heart's deep core,
But a plea, that upward to Heaven he flings—
I know why the caged bird sings!

○

FROM AUGURIES OF INNOCENCE

WILLIAM BLAKE

To see a world in a Grain of Sand
And a Heaven in a Wild Flower,
Hold Infinity in the palm of your hand
And Eternity in an hour.

And Robin Red Breast in a Cage
Puts all Heaven in a Rage.

A dove house filled with doves and Pigeons
Shudders Hell through all its regions.
A dog starved at his Master's Gate
Predicts the ruin of the State.
A horse misus'd upon the Road
Calls to Heaven for Human blood.
Each outcry from the hunted hare
A fiber from the Brain does tear.
A skylark wounded in the wing,
A Cerubim does cease to sing.
. . . .

He who shall hurt the little Wren
Shall never be beloved by Men.
. . . .

The wanton Boy that kills the Fly
Shall feel the Spider's enmity.
. . . .

Kill not the Moth or Butterfly,
For the Last Judgment draweth nigh.
. . . .

The Beggar's Dog and Widow's Cat,
Feed them & thou wilt grow fat.

◌

DOG ON A CHAIN
CHARLES SIMIC

So, that's how it's going to be
A cold day smelling of snow
Step around the bare oak tree
And see how quickly you get
Yourself entangled for good.
Your bad luck was being friendly
With people who love their new couch
More than they love you.

Fred, you poor mutt, the night
Is falling. The children playing
Across the road were cold,
So they ran in. Watch the smoke
Swirl out of their chimney
In the windy sky as long as you can.
Soon, no one will see you there.
You'll have to bark even if
There's no moon, bark and growl
To keep yourself company.

○

SAINT FRANCIS AND THE SOW

GALWAY KINNELL

The bud
stands for all things,
even for those things that don't flower,
for everything flowers, from within, of self-blessing;
though sometimes it is necessary
to reteach a thing its loveliness,
to put hand on its brow
of the flower
and retell it in words and in touch
it is lovely
until it flowers again from within, of self-blessing;
as Saint Francis
put his hand on the creased forehead
of the sow, and told her in words and in touch
blessings of earth on the sow, and the sow
began remembering all down her thick length,
from the earthen snout all the way
through the fodder and slops to the spiritual curl of the tail,
from the hard spininess spiked out from the spine
down through the great broken heart

to the sheer blue milken dreaminess spurting and shuddering
from the fourteen teats into the fourteen mouths sucking
   and blowing beneath them:
the long, perfect loveliness of sow.

○

A RABBIT AS KING OF THE GHOSTS
WALLACE STEVENS

The difficulty to think at the end of day,
When the shapeless shadow covers the sun
And nothing is left except light on your fur—

There was the cat slopping its milk all day,
Fat cat, red tongue, green mind, white milk
And August the most peaceful month.

To be, in the grass, in the peacefullest time,
Without that monument of cat,
The cat forgotten in the moon;

And to feel that the light is a rabbit-light,
In which everything is meant for you
And nothing need be explained;

Then there is nothing to think of. It comes of itself;
And east rushes west and west rushes down,
No matter. The grass is full

And full of yourself. The trees around are for you,
The whole of the wideness of night is for you,
A self that touches all edges,

You become a self that fills the four corners of night.
The red cat hides away in the fur-light
And there you are humped high, humped up,

You are humped higher and higher, black as stone—
You sit with your head like a carving in space
And the little green cat is a bug in the grass.

○

HAST THOU GIVEN THE HORSE STRENGTH?
FROM THE KING JAMES VERSION OF THE BIBLE, JOB 39:25

Hast thou given the horse strength?
Hast thou clothed his neck with thunder?
Canst thou make him afraid as a grasshopper?
The glory of his nostrils is terrible.
He paweth in the valley, and rejoiceth in his strength;
He goeth on to meet the armed men.
He swalloweth the ground with fierceness and rage;
Neither believeth he that it is the sound of the trumpet.
He saith among the trumpets, "Ha, Ha!"
And he smelleth the battle afar off,
The thunder of the captains, and the shouting.

○

A STALLION
WALT WHITMAN

A gigantic beauty of a stallion, fresh and responsive to my caresses,
Head high in the forehead, wide between the ears,
Limbs glossy and supple, tail dusting the ground,
Eyes full of sparkling wickedness, ears finely cut, flexibly moving.

His nostrils dilate as my heels embrace him,
His well-built limbs tremble with pleasure as we race around and
    return.

I but use you a minute, then I resign you, stallion,
Why do I need your paces when I myself out-gallop them?
Even as I stand or sit passing faster than you.

A Blessing

JAMES WRIGHT

Just off the highway to Rochester, Minnesota,
Twilight bounds softly forth on the grass.
And the eyes of those two Indian ponies
Darken with kindness.
They have come gladly out of the willows
To welcome my friend and me.

We step over the barbed wire into the pasture
Where they have been grazing all day, alone.
They ripple tensely, they can hardly contain their happiness
That we have come.
They bow shyly as wet swans. They love each other.
There is no loneliness like theirs.
At home once more,
They begin munching the young tufts of spring in the
    darkness.
I would like to hold the slenderer one in my arms,
For she has walked over to me
And nuzzled my left hand.
She is black and white,
Her mane falls wild on her forehead,
And the light breeze moves me to caress her long ear
That is delicate as the skin over a girl's wrist.
Suddenly I realize
That if I stepped out of my body I would break
Into blossom.

THE FISH

ELIZABETH BISHOP

I caught a tremendous fish
and held him beside the boat
half out of water, with my hook
fast in a corner of his mouth.
He didn't fight.
He hadn't fought at all.
He hung a grunting weight,
battered and venerable
and homely. Here and there
his brown skin hung in strips
like ancient wallpaper,
and its pattern of darker brown
was like wallpaper:
shapes like full-blown roses
stained and lost through age.
He was speckled with barnacles,
fine rosettes of lime,
and infested
with tiny white sea-lice,
and underneath two or three
rags of green weed hung down.
While his gills were breathing in
the terrible oxygen
—the frightening gills,
fresh and crisp with blood,
that can cut so badly—
I thought of the coarse white flesh
packed in like feathers,
the big bones and the little bones,
the dramatic reds and blacks
of his shiny entrails,
and the pink swim-bladder
like a big peony.

I looked into his eyes
which were far larger than mine
but shallower, and yellowed,
the irises backed and packed
with tarnished tinfoil
seen through the lenses
of old scratched isinglass.
They shifted a little, but not
to return my stare.
—It was more like the tipping
of an object toward the light.
I admired his sullen face,
the mechanism of his jaw,
and then I saw
that from his lower lip
—if you could call it a lip—
grim, wet, and weaponlike,
hung five old pieces of fish-line,
or four and a wire leader
with the swivel still attached,
with all their five big hooks
grown firmly in his mouth.
A green line, frayed at the end
where he broke it, two heavier lines,
and a fine black thread
still crimped from the strain and snap
when it broke and he got away.
Like medals with their ribbons
frayed and wavering,
a five-haired beard of wisdom
trailing from his aching jaw.
I stared and stared
and victory filled up
the little rented boat,
from the pool of bilge
where oil had spread a rainbow

around the rusted engine
to the bailer rusted orange,
the sun-cracked thwarts,
the oarlocks on their strings,
the gunnels—until everything
was rainbow, rainbow, rainbow!
And I let the fish go.

◎

LITTLE THINGS
JAMES STEPHENS

Little things, that run, and quail,
And die, in silence and despair!

Little things, that fight, and fail,
And fall, on sea, and earth, and air!

All trapped and frightened little things,
The mouse, the coney, hear our prayer!

As we forgive those done to us,
—The lamb, the linnet, and the hare—

Forgive us all our trespasses,
Little creatures, everywhere!

◎

HURT NO LIVING THING
CHRISTINA GEORGINA ROSSETTI

Hurt no living thing:
Ladybird, no butterfly,
Nor moth with dusty wing,
No cricket chirping cheerily,
Nor grasshopper so light of leap,
Nor dancing gnat, nor beetle fat,
Nor harmless worms that creep.

VI
Seasons of the Year

All seasons may be sweet to thee

—*SAMUEL TAYLOR COLERIDGE TO HIS SLEEPING*

INFANT DAUGHTER.

IN A PASSEL OF TREES WHERE THE BRANCHES
TRAPPED THE WIND INTO WHISTLING, "WHO? WHO ARE YOU?"

THE GRASS ON THE MOUNTAIN

FROM THE PAIUTE, NATIVE AMERICAN
TRANSCRIBED BY MARY AUSTIN

Oh, long long
The snow has possessed the mountains.

The deer have come down and the big-horn,
They have followed the Sun to the south
To feed on the mesquite pods and the bunch grass.
Loud are the thunderdrums
In the tents of the mountains.
Oh, long long
Have we eaten chia seeds
And dried deer's flesh of the summer killing.
We are wearied of our huts
And the smoky smell of our garments.

We are sick with desire of the sun
And the grass on the mountain.

○

SING UNTO THE LORD WITH THANKSGIVING

FROM THE KING JAMES VERSION OF THE BIBLE, PSALM 147: 7–8

Sing unto the Lord with thanksgiving;
Sing praises upon the harp unto our God:
Who covereth the heaven with clouds,
Who prepareth rain for the earth,
Who maketh grass to grow upon the mountains.

MY BELOVED SPAKE, AND SAID UNTO ME

FROM THE KING JAMES VERSION OF THE BIBLE, SONG OF SOLOMON 1:10–13,

My beloved spake, and said unto me, Rise up, my love, my fair one,
    and come away.
For, lo, the winter is past, the rain is over and gone;
The flowers appear on the earth; the time of the singing of the
    birds is come, and the voice of the turtle is heard in our land;
The fig tree putteth forth her green figs, and the vines with the
    tender grapes give a good smell. Arise, my love, my fair one, and
    come away.

LOVELIEST OF TREES, THE CHERRY NOW

A. E. HOUSMAN

Loveliest of trees, the cherry now
Is hung with bloom along the bough,
And stands about the woodland ride
Wearing white for Eastertide.

Now, of my threescore years and ten,
Twenty will not come again,
And take from seventy springs a score,
It only leaves me fifty more.

And since to look at things in bloom
Fifty springs are little room,
About the woodlands I will go
To see the cherry hung with snow.

IN JUST-

E. E. CUMMINGS

in Just-
spring   when the world is mud-
luscious the little
lame balloonman

whistles   far   and wee

and eddieandbill come
running from marbles and

piracies and it's
spring

when the world is puddle-wonderful

the queer
old balloonman whistles
far   and   wee
and bettyandisbel come dancing

from hop-scotch and jump-rope and

it's
spring
and
        the

          goat-footed
balloonMan   whistles
far
and
wee

THE FIRST DANDELION

FROM LEAVES OF GRASS
WALT WHITMAN

Simple and fresh and fair from winter's close emerging,
As if no artifice of fashion, business, politics, had ever been,
Forth from its sunny nook of shelter'd grass—innocent, golden,
    calm as the dawn,
The spring's first dandelion shows its trustful face.

            ◎

DAFFODILS

WILLIAM WORDSWORTH

I wandered lonely as a cloud
That floats on high o'er vales and hills,
When all at once I saw a crowd,
A host, of golden daffodils;
Beside the lake, beneath the trees,
Fluttering and dancing in the breeze.

Continuous as the stars that shine
And twinkle on the milky way,
They stretched in never-ending line
Along the margin of a bay:
Ten thousand saw I at a glance,
Tossing their heads in sprightly dance.

The waves beside them danced; but they
Out-did the sparkling waves in glee:
A poet could not be gay,
In such a jocund company:
I gazed—and gazed—but little thought
What wealth the show to me had brought;

For oft, when on my couch I lie
In vacant or in pensive mood,
They flash upon that inward eye
Which is the bliss of solitude;
And then my heart with pleasure fills,
And dances with the daffodils.

○

AT THE SEASIDE
ROBERT LOUIS STEVENSON

When I was down beside the sea
A wooden spade they gave to me
   To dig the sandy shore.
My holes were empty like a cup,
In every hole the sea came up,
   Till it could come no more.

○

MAGGIE AND MILLY AND MOLLY AND MAY
E. E. CUMMINGS

maggie and milly and molly and may
went down to the beach(to play one day)

and maggie discovered a shell that sang
so sweetly she couldn't remember her troubles,and

milly befriended a stranded star
whose ray five languid fingers were;

and molly was chased by a horrible thing
which raced sideways while blowing bubbles:and

may came home with a smooth round stone
as small as a world and as large as alone.

For whatever we lose(like a you or a me)
it's always ourselves we find in the sea

WIND SONG

CARL SANDBURG

Long ago I learned how to sleep,
In an old apple orchard where the wind swept by counting
    its money and throwing it away,
In a wind-gaunt orchard where the limbs forked out and listened or
    never listened at all,
In a passel of trees where the branches trapped the wind into
    whistling,
  "Who, who are you?"
I slept with my head in an elbow on a summer afternoon
    and there I took a sleep lesson.
There I went away saying: I know why they sleep, I know
    how they trap the tricky winds.
Long ago I learned how to listen to the singing wind and
    how to forget and how to hear the deep whine,
Slapping and lapsing under the day blue and the night stars: Who,
    who are you?

      Who can ever forget
      listening to the wind go by
      counting its money
      and throwing it away?

◎

AUGUST

FEDERICO GARCIA LORCA

The opposing
of peach and sugar,
and the sun inside the afternoon
like the stone in the fruit

The ear of corn keeps
its laughter intact, yellow and firm

August.
The little boys eat
brown bread and delicious moon.

○

END-OF-SUMMER POEM
ROWENA BASTIN BENNETT

The little songs of summer are all gone today.
The little insect instruments are all packed away:
The bumblebee's snare drum, the grasshopper's guitar
The katydid's castanets—I wonder where they are.
The bullfrog's banjo, the cricket's violin,
The dragonfly's cello have ceased their merry din.
Oh, where is the orchestra? From harpist down to drummer,
They've all disappeared with the passing of the summer.

○

BLACKBERRY EATING
GALWAY KINNELL

I love to go out in late September
among the fat, overripe, icy, black blackberries
to eat blackberries for breakfast,
the stalks very prickly, a penalty
they earn for knowing the black art
of blackberry-making; and as I stand among them
lifting the stalks to my mouth, the ripest berries
fall almost unbidden to my tongue,
as words sometimes do, certain peculiar words
like strengths or squinched,
many-lettered, one-syllabled lumps,
which I squeeze, squinch open, and splurge well
in the silent, startled, icy, black language
of blackberry—eating in late September.

CHRYSALIS DIARY

FROM JOYFUL NOISE: POEMS FOR 2 VOICES
PAUL FLEISCHMAN

November 13:

Cold told me
to fasten my feet
to this branch,

to dangle upside down
from my perch,

to shed my skin,

to cease being a caterpillar
and I have obeyed.

and I have obeyed.

December 6:

Green,

the color of leaves and life,
has vanished!

has vanished!
The empire of leaves
lies in ruins!

lies in ruins!
I study the
brown new world around me.

I fear the future.

I hear few sounds.

Have any others of my kind
survived this cataclysm?

Swinging back and forth
in the wind,
I feel immeasurably alone.

January 4:

I can make out snow falling.

For five days and nights
it's been drifting down.

I find I never tire of
watching the flakes
in their multitudes
passing my window.

Astounding.
I enter these
wondrous events
in my chronicle

The world is now white.
Astounding.

knowing no reader
would believe me.

February 12:

An ice storm last night.

Unable to see out
at all this morning.

Yet I hear boughs cracking

and branches falling.

Hungry for sounds
in this silent world,
I cherish these,

ponder their import,

miser them away
in my memory,

and wait for more.

and wait for more.

March 28:

I wonder whether
I am the same being
who started this diary.

like the weather without.

I've felt stormy inside

my legs are dissolving,

My mouth is reshaping,

wings are growing
my body's not mine.

my body's not mine.

This morning,
a breeze from the south,
strangely fragrant,

a red-winged blackbird's
call in the distance,

a faint glimpse of green
in the branches.

And now I recall
that last night
I dreamt of flying.

◯

SOMETHING TOLD THE WILD GEESE
RACHEL FIELD

Something told the wild geese
It was time to go.
Though the fields lay golden,
Something whispered
                    Snow.

Leaves were green and stirring,
Berries luster-glossed.
But beneath warm feathers,
Something cautioned
                    Frost.

All the dangling orchards
Steamed with sweet and spice.
But each wild breast stiffened
At remembered
                    Ice.

Something told the wild geese
It was time to fly—
Summer sun was on their wings,
                    Winter in their cry.

THANKSGIVING POEM

ARTHUR GREEN

The crops we planted in the spring
Have come into their full being.

The fat, flat little pumpkin seed
Is now a pumpkin in its stead.

The kernel dropped into the ground
Is a stout stalk with ears all round.

> And all this squash
> Is just too much!

November has encumbered us
With all of these cucumbers plus

Eggplant slender as a snake
And eggplant that is eggplant-shaped.

Take some! Please do! O, take some, please!
Take mustard greens and crowder peas!

> These carrots, too!
> This honey dew!

'Taters, 'matoes, beans with strings
And beans without 'em! our blessings!

Of kale and turnips there's no dirth!
Our gratitude to Mother Earth!

The hope hid in our hearts last spring
Has now become our Thanksgiving!

Hanukah Poem

ARTHUR GREEN

In the darkest winter nights
We celebrate the Feast of Lights!
First one, then there are two—
Each night of Hanukah a new

Until every candle's lit
And all the joy that goes with it
Is ours to share as we recall
The miracle of the blessed oil:

How wicked old Antiochus
Did such evil things to us—
Spoiled the Temple,
Spilled the oil—

All but a tiny little bit—
Just enough to keep it lit
For one short night.
And yet, for eight the flame burned bright!

So now, within the candles' glow
    On this our festival of lights,
Our loving faces happy show
    Even in the darkest nights

As we dance and play and sing,
This miracle remembering.

THE CHERRY-TREE CAROL
OLD ENGLISH CAROL

Joseph was an old man,
   and an old man was he,
When he wedded Mary,
   in the land of Galilee.

Joseph and Mary walked
   through an orchard good,
Where was cherries and berries,
   so red as any blood.

O then bespoke Mary,
   so meek and so mild:
"Pluck me one cherry, Joseph,
   for I am with child."

O then bespoke Joseph,
   with words most unkind:
"Let him pluck thee a cherry
   that brought thee with child."

O then bespoke the babe,
   within his mother's womb:
"Bow down then the tallest tree,
   for my mother to have some."

Then bowed down the highest tree
   unto his mother's hand;
Then she cried, "See, Joseph,
   I have cherries at command."

Then Mary plucked a cherry,
   as red as the blood,
Then Mary went home
   with her heavy load.

A Visit from St. Nicholas

CLEMENT CLARKE MOORE

'Twas the night before Christmas, when all thro' the house,
Not a creature was stirring, not even a mouse;
The stockings were hung by the chimney with care,
In hopes that St. Nicholas soon would be there;
The children were nestled all snug in their beds,
While visions of sugar plums danc'd in their heads,
And Mama in her 'kerchief, and I in my cap,
Had just settled down for a long winter's nap—
When out on the lawn there arose such a clatter,
I sprang from the bed to see what was the matter.
Away to the window I flew like a flash,
Tore open the shutters, and threw up the sash.
The moon on the breast of the new fallen snow,
Gave the luster of mid-day to objects below;
When, what to my wondering eyes should appear,
But a miniature sleigh, and eight tiny rein-deer,
With a little old driver, so lively and quick,
I knew in a moment that it must be St. Nick.
More rapid than eagles his coursers they came,
And he whistled, and shouted, and call'd them by name:
"Now! Dasher, now! Dancer, now! Prancer, and Vixen,
On! Comet, on! Cupid, on! Donner and Blitzen;
To the top of the porch! to the top of the wall!
Now dash away! dash away! dash away all!"
As dry leaves before the wild hurricane fly,
When they meet with an obstacle, mount to the sky;
So up to the house-top the coursers they flew,
With the sleigh full of Toys—and St. Nicholas too:
And then in a twinkling, I heard on the roof
The prancing and pawing of each little hoof.
As I drew in my head, and was turning around,
Down the chimney St. Nicholas came with a bound:
He was dress'd all in fur, from his head to his foot,

137

And his clothes were all tarnish'd with ashes and soot;
A bundle of toys was flung on his back,
And he look'd like a peddler just opening his pack:
His eyes—how they twinkled! his dimples how merry,
His cheeks were like roses, his nose like a cherry;
His droll little mouth was drawn up like a bow,
And the beard of his chin was as white as the snow;
The stump of a pipe he held tight in his teeth,
And the smoke it encircled his head like a wreath.
He had a broad face, and a little round belly
That shook when he laugh'd, like a bowl full of jelly:
He was chubby and plump, a right jolly old elf,
And I laugh'd when I saw him in spite of myself;
A wink of his eye and a twist of his head
Soon gave me to know I had nothing to dread.
He spoke not a word, but went straight to his work,
And fill'd all the stockings; then turn'd with a jerk,
And laying his finger aside of his nose
And giving a nod, up the chimney he rose.
He sprung to his sleigh, to his team gave a whistle,
And away they all flew, like the down of a thistle:
But I heard him exclaim, ere he drove out of sight—
"Happy Christmas to all, and to all a good night."

○

JANUARY
LUCILLE CLIFTON

"Walk tall in the world"
  says Mama
  to Everett Anderson.
"The year is new and
  so are the days,
  walk tall in the world,"
  she says.

PIPED A TINY VOICE NEAR BY
RALPH WALDO EMERSON

Piped a tiny voice near by,
Gay and polite, a cheerful cry—
Chick-chick-a-dee-de! Saucy note
Out of sound heart and merry throat,
As if it said, "Good-day, good Sir!
Fine afternoon, old passenger!
Happy to meet you in these places
Where January brings few faces."

○

VELVET SHOES
ELINOR WYLIE

Let us walk in the white snow
   In a soundless space;
With footsteps quiet and slow,
    At a tranquil pace,
    Under veils of white lace.

I shall go shod in silk,
   And you in wool,
White as a white cow's milk,
    More beautiful
    Than the breast of a gull.

We shall walk through the still town
   In a windless peace;
We shall step upon white down,
    Upon silver fleece,
    Upon softer than these.

We shall walk in velvet shoes:
　　Wherever we go
Silence will fall like dews
　　On white silence below.
　　We shall walk in the snow.

○

WHEN ICICLES HANG BY THE WALL
FROM LOVE'S LABOR'S LOST, *ACT V, SCENE II*
WILLIAM SHAKESPEARE

When icicles hang by the wall,
　　And Dick the shepherd blows his nail,
And Tom bears logs into the hall,
　　And milk comes frozen home in pail,
When blood is nipped and ways be foul,
Then nightly sings the staring owl,
　　"Tu-whit, tu-whoo!" A merry note,
While greasy Joan doth keel the pot.

When all aloud the wind doth blow,
　　And coughing drowns the parson's saw,
And birds sit brooding in the snow,
　　And Marian's nose looks red and raw;
When roasted crabs hiss in the bowl,
Then nightly sings the staring owl,
　　"Tu-whit, tu-whoo!" A merry note,
While greasy Joan doth keel the pot.

UNDER THE GREENWOOD TREE

FROM AS YOU LIKE IT, *ACT II, SCENE IV*
WILLIAM SHAKESPEARE

Under the greenwood tree
Who loves to lie with me,
And turn his merry note
Unto the sweet bird's throat,
Come hither, come hither, come hither:
Here shall he see
No enemy
But winter and rough weather.

Who doth ambition shun,
And loves to live i' the sun,
Seeking the food he eats,
And pleased with what he gets,
Come hither, come hither, come hither:
Here shall he see
No enemy
But winter and rough weather.

CHILDREN BORN OF FAIRY STOCK / NEVER NEED FOR SHIRT OR FROCK.

VII
Fairies, Witches, Goblins & Company

They live on cherries, they run wild—
I'd love to be a Fairy's child.

—*ROBERT GRAVES*

O TO BE A DRAGON

MARIANNE MOORE

> If I, like Solomon, ...
> could have my wish—

my wish ... O to be a dragon,
a symbol of the power of Heaven—of silkworm
size or immense; at times invisible.
> Felicitous phenomenon!

◎

THE SALIVA OF A DRAGON

ANCIENT CHINESE SCHOLARS

The saliva of a dragon produces all kinds of perfume!

◎

I'D LOVE TO BE A FAIRY'S CHILD

ROBERT GRAVES

Children born of fairy stock
Never need for shirt or frock,
Never want for food or fire,
Always get their heart's desire:
Jingle pockets full of gold,
Marry when they're seven years old.
Every fairy child may keep
Two strong ponies and ten sheep;
All have houses, each his own,
Built of brick or granite stone;
They live on cherries, they run wild—
I'd love to be a Fairy's child.

GOBLIN FEET

J. R. R. TOLKIEN

I am off down the road
Where the fairy lanterns glowed
And the little pretty flitter-mice are flying:
A slender bank of gray
It runs creepily away
And the hedges and the grasses are a-sighing.
The air is full of wings,
And of blundery beetle-things
That warn you with their whirring and their humming.
O! I hear the tiny horns
Of enchanted leprechauns
And the padded feet of many gnomes a-coming!

O! the lights! O! the gleams! O! the little tinkly sounds!
O! the rustle of their noiseless little robes!
O! the echo of their feet—of their happy little feet!
O! their swinging lamps in little starlit globes.

I must follow in their train
Down the crooked fairy lane
Where the coney-rabbits long ago have gone,
And where silvery they sing
In a moving moonlit ring
All a-twinkle with the jewels they have on.
They are fading round the turn
Where the glow-worms palely burn
And the echo of their padding feet is dying!
O! it's knocking at my heart—
Let me go! O! let me start!
For the little magic hours are all a-flying.

O! the warmth! O! the hum! O! the colours in the dark!
O! the gauzy wings of golden honey-flies!
O! the music of their feet—of their dancing goblin feet!
O! the magic! O! the sorrow when it dies.

CHIP THE GLASSES AND CRACK THE PLATES!

FROM THE HOBBIT
J. R. R. TOLKIEN

Chip the glasses and crack the plates!
    Blunt the knives and bend the forks!
That's what Bilbo Baggins hates!
    Smash the bottles and burn the corks!

Cut the cloth and tread on the fat!
    Pour the milk on the pantry floor!
Leave the bones on the bedroom mat!
    Splash the wine on every door!

Dump the crocks in a boiling bowl;
    Pound them up with a thumping pole;
And when you are finished, if any are whole,
    Send them down the hall to roll!

That's what Bilbo Baggins hates!
So, carefully! carefully with the plates!

◎

THE BAD KITTENS

ELIZABETH COATSWORTH

You may call, you may call,
But the little black cats won't hear you,
The little black cats are maddened
By the bright green light of the moon,
They are whirling and running and hiding.
They are wild who were once so confiding,
They are crazed when the moon is riding—
You will not catch the kittens soon.
They care not for saucers of milk,
They think not of pillows of silk,
Your softest, crooningest call
Is less than the buzzing of flies.

They are seeing more than you see,
They are hearing more than you hear,
And out of the darkness they peer
With a goblin light in their eyes.

○

OVERHEARD ON A SALTMARSH
HAROLD MONRO

Nymph, nymph, what are your beads?

Green glass, goblin. Why do you stare at them?

Give them me.
                  No.
Give them me. Give them me.
                             No.
Then I will howl all night in the reeds,
Lie in the mud and howl for them.

Goblin, why do you love them so?

They are better than stars or water,
Better than voices of winds that sing,
Better than any man's fair daughter,
Your green glass beads on a silver ring.

Hush, I stole them out of the moon.

Give me your beads, I want them.
                        No.

I will howl in a deep lagoon
For your green glass beads, I love them so.
Give them me. Give them.
                  No.

HOW TO TELL GOBLINS FROM ELVES

MONICA SHANNON

The Goblin has a wider mouth
    Than any wondering elf.
The saddest part of this is that
    He brings it on himself.
For hanging in a willow clump
    In baskets made of sheaves,
You may see the baby goblins
    Under coverlets of leaves.

They suck a pink and podgy foot,
    (As human babies do),
And then they suck the other one,
    Until they're sucking two.
And so it is that goblins' mouths
    Keep growing very round.
So you can't mistake a goblin,
    When a goblin you have found.

○

THE ELF AND THE DORMOUSE

OLIVER HERFORD

Under a toadstool
    Crept a wee Elf,
Out of the rain
    To shelter himself.

Under the toadstool,
    Sound asleep,
Sat a big Dormouse
    All in a heap.

Trembled the wee Elf,
    Frightened, and yet
Fearing to fly away
    Lest he get wet.

To the next shelter—
    Maybe a mile!
Sudden the wee Elf
    Smiled a wee smile,

Tugged till the toadstool
    Toppled in two.
Holding it over him
    Gaily he flew.

Soon he was safe home
    Dry as could be.
Soon woke the Dormouse—
    "Good gracious me!

Where is my toadstool?"
    Loud he lamented.
—And that's how umbrellas
    First were invented.

◉

THE GNOME
HARRY BEHN

I saw a Gnome
As plain as plain
Sitting on top
Of a weathervane.

He was dressed like a crow
In silky black feathers,
And there he sat watching
All kinds of weathers.

He talked like a crow too,
Caw caw caw,
When he told me exactly
What he saw,

Snow to the north of him
Sun to the south,
And he spoke with a beaky
Kind of a mouth.

But he wasn't a crow,
That was plain as plain
'Cause crows never sit
On a weathervane.

What I saw was simply
A usual gnome
Looking things over
On his way home.

○

FROM THE BROOMSTICK TRAIN
OLIVER WENDELL HOLMES

Look out! Look out, boys! Clear the track!
The witches are here! They've all come back!
They hanged them high,—No use! No use!
What cares a witch for the hangman's noose!
They buried them deep, but they wouldn't lie still,
For cats and witches are hard to kill;
They swore they shouldn't and wouldn't die,—
Books said they did, but they lie! they lie!

○

THE RIDE-BY-NIGHTS
WALTER DE LA MARE

Up on their brooms the Witches stream,
Crooked and black in the crescent's gleam,
One foot high, and one foot low,
Bearded, cloaked, and cowled, they go.

'Neath Charlie's Wane they twitter and tweet,
And away they swarm 'neath the Dragon's feet,
With a whoop and a flutter they swing and sway,
And surge pell-mell down the Milky Way.
Between the legs of the glittering Chair
They hover and squeak in the empty air.

Then round they swoop past the glimmering Lion
To where Sirius barks behind huge Orion;
Up, then, and over to wheel amain
Under the silver, and home again.

○

THE FAIRIES
ROBERT HERRICK

If ye will with Mab find grace,
Set each platter in his place;
Rake the fire up, and get
Water in, ere sun be set.
Wash your pails and cleanse your dairies,
Sluts are loathsome to the fairies;
Sweep your house: Who doth not so,
Mab will pinch her by the toe.

○

OH, THEN, I SEE QUEEN MAB HATH BEEN WITH YOU
FROM ROMEO AND JULIET, ACT I, SCENE IV
WILLIAM SHAKESPEARE

Oh, then, I see Queen Mab hath been with you.
She is the fairies' midwife, and she comes
In shape no bigger than an agate stone
On the forefinger of an alderman,
Drawn with a team of little atomies
Athwart men's noses as they lie asleep;

Her wagon spokes made of long spinners' legs,
The cover of the wings of grasshoppers,
The traces of the smallest spider's web,
The collars of the moonshine's watery beams,
Her whip of cricket's bone, the lash of film,
Her wagoner a small, gray-coated gnat,
Not half so big as a round little worm
Prick'd from the lazy finger of a maid;
Her chariot is an empty hazelnut
Made by the joiner squirrel or old grub,
Time out o' mind the fairies' coachmakers.

And in this state she gallops night by night
Through lovers' brains, and then they dream of love;
O'er courtiers' knees, that dream in court'sies straight;
O'er lawyers' fingers, who straight dream in fees;
O'er ladies' lips, who straight on kisses dream,
Which oft the angry Mab with blisters plagues,
Because their breaths with sweetmeats tainted are.
Sometimes she gallops o'er a courtier's nose,
And then he dreams of smelling out a suit;
And sometimes comes she with a tithe pig's tail
Tickling a parson's nose as he lies asleep,
Then dreams he of another benefice.

Sometimes she driveth o'er a soldier's neck,
And then dreams he of cutting foreign throats,
Of breaches, ambuscades, Spanish blades,
Of healths five fathoms deep; and then anon
Drums in his ear, at which he starts and wakes,
And being thus frighted swears a prayer or two
And sleeps again. This is that very Mab
That plaits the manes of horses in the night
And bakes the elf locks in foul sluttish hairs,
Which once untangled much misfortune bodes,
This is she.

DOUBLE, DOUBLE, TOIL AND TROUBLE
FROM MACBETH, ACT IV, SCENE I
WILLIAM SHAKESPEARE

First Witch. Thrice the brinded cat hath mew'd.

Sec. Witch. Thrice and once the hedge-pig whined.

Third Witch. Harpier cries "'Tis time, 'tis time."

First Witch. Round about the cauldron go:
    In the poison'd entrails throw.
    Toad, that under cold stone
    Days and nights has thirty one
    Swelter'd venom sleeping got,
    Boil thou first i' the charmed pot.

All. Double, double, toil and trouble;
    Fire burn and cauldron bubble.

Sec. Witch. Fillet of a fenny snake,
    In the cauldron boil and bake;
    Eye of newt and toe of frog,
    Wool of bat and tongue of dog,
    Adder's fork and blind-worm's sting,
    Lizard's leg and howlet's wing,
    For a charm of powerful trouble,
    Like a hell-broth boil and bubble.

All. Double, double, toil and trouble;
    Fire burn and cauldron bubble.

Third Witch. Scale of dragon, tooth of wolf,
    Witches' mummy, maw and gulf
    Of the ravin'd salt-sea shark,
    Root of hemlock digg'd i' the dark,

All. Double, double, toil and trouble
    Fire burn and cauldron bubble.

Sec. Witch. Cool it with a baboon's blood,
    Then the charm is firm and good.

FAIRIES' SONG

FROM A MIDSUMMER NIGHT'S DREAM, *ACT II, SCENE II*
WILLIAM SHAKESPEARE

FIRST FAIRY

You spotted snakes with double tongue,
    Thorny hedgehogs be not seen;
Newts, and blind-worms, do no wrong;
    Come not near our fairy queen.

    Philomel with melody
    Sing in our sweet lullaby;
Lulla, lulla, lullaby; lulla, lulla, lullaby!
Never harm, nor spell, nor charm,
    Come our lovely lady nigh!
    So good-night, with lullaby.

SECOND FAIRY

Weaving spiders, come not here;
    Hence, you long-legged spinners, hence;
Beetles black, approach not near;
    Worm, nor snail, do no offense.

    Philomel with melody
    Sing in our sweet lullaby;
Lulla, lulla, lullaby; lulla, lulla, lullaby!
Never harm, nor spell, nor charm,
    Come our lovely lady nigh!
    So good-night, with lullaby.

THE FAIRY'S FUNERAL

WILLIAM BLAKE

"Did you ever see a fairy's funeral?" said Blake to a lady who
sat next to him at some gathering…"Never, Sir," was the
answer. "I have," he replied, "but not before last night. I was
writing alone in my garden; there was a great stillness among
the branches and flowers, and more than common sweetness
in the air; I heard a low and pleasant sound, and I knew not
whence it came. At last I saw the broad leaf of a flower move,
and underneath I saw a procession of creatures of the size and
color of green and gray grasshoppers, bearing a body laid out on
a rose leaf, which they buried with songs and disappeared."

○

SOMEONE

WALTER DE LA MARE

Someone came knocking
    At my wee, small door;
Someone came knocking,
    I'm sure—sure—sure;
I listened, I opened,
    I looked to left and right,
But nought there was a-stirring
    In the still, dark night;
Only the busy beetle
    Tap-tapping in the wall,
Only from the forest
    The screech owl's call,
Only the cricket whistling
    While the dewdrops fall,
So I know not who came knocking,
    At all, at all, at all.

The Listeners

WALTER DE LA MARE

"Is there anybody there?" said the Traveler,
　　Knocking on the moonlit door;
And his horse in the silence champed the grasses
　　Of the forest's ferny floor.
And a bird flew up out of the turret,
　　Above the Traveler's head:
And he smote upon the door again a second time;
　　"Is there anybody there?" he said.
But no one descended to the Traveler;
　　No head from the leaf-fringed sill
Leaned over and looked into his gray eyes,
　　Where he stood perplexed and still.
But only a host of phantom listeners
　　That dwelt in the lone house then
Stood listening in the quiet of the moonlight
　　To that voice from the world of men:
Stood thronging the faint moonbeams on the dark stair
　　That goes down to the empty hall,
Hearkening in an air stirred and shaken
　　By the lonely Traveler's call.
And he felt in his heart their strangeness,
　　Their stillness answering his cry,
While his horse moved, cropping the dark turf,
　　'Neath the starred and leafy sky;
For he suddenly smote on the door, even
　　Louder, and lifted his head:—
"Tell them I came, and no one answered,
　　That I kept my word," he said.
Never the least stir made the listeners,
　　Though every word he spake
Fell echoing through the shadowiness of the still house
　　From the one man left awake:

Aye, they heard his foot upon the stirrup,
  And the sound of iron on stone,
And how the silence surged softly backward,
  When the plunging hoofs were gone.

○

WINDY NIGHTS

ROBERT LOUIS STEVENSON

Whenever the moon and stars are set,
  Whenever the wind is high,
All night long in the dark and wet,
  A man goes riding by.
Late in the night when the fires are out,
  Why does he gallop and gallop about?

Whenever the trees are crying aloud,
  And ships are tossed at sea,
By, on the highway, low and loud,
  By at the gallop goes he.
By at the gallop he goes, and then
  By he comes back at the gallop again.

○

THE FEATHERY MAN

Ho, hoo! I know who I am—
I'm the poor little, poor little
Feathery Man.

Ho, hoo! I know whence I came—
I came from the woods
And I go thence again.

Ho, hoo! O who was my dam?
My sire was the hoot-owl,
A ghost was my ma'am.

Ho, hoo! O what is my name?
Sorrow, sing sorrow,
My name is the same.

Whip-Poor-Will! Whip-Poor-Will!
Whip-Poor-Will! Whip-Poor-Will!

○

ARIEL'S SONG
FROM THE TEMPEST, *ACT V, SCENE I*
WILLIAM SHAKESPEARE

Where the bee sucks, there suck I:
In a cowslips bell I lie;
There I couch when owls do cry.
On the bat's back I do fly
After summer merrily.
Merrily, merrily shall I live now
Under the blossom that hangs on the bough.

○

CALIBAN'S ENTREATY
FROM THE TEMPEST, *ACT II, SCENE II*
WILLIAM SHAKESPEARE

I prithee, let me bring thee where crabs grow;
And I with my long nails will dig thee pig-nuts;
Show thee a jay's nest, and instruct thee how
To snare the nimble marmoset; I'll bring thee
To clustering filberts, and sometimes I'll get thee
Young scamels from the rock. Wilt thou go with me?

CALIBAN'S ADVICE

FROM THE TEMPEST, *ACT III, SCENE II*
WILLIAM SHAKESPEARE

Be not afeard: the isle is full of noises,

Sounds and sweet airs, that give delight, and hurt not.

Sometimes a thousand twangling instruments

Will hum about mine ears; and sometimes voices,

That, if I then had wak'd after long sleep,

Will make me sleep again: and then, in dreaming,

The clouds methought would open and show riches

Ready to drop upon me; that, when I wak'd

I cried to dream again.

○

THE WIND BLOWS OUT OF THE GATES OF THE DAY

FROM THE LAND OF HEART'S DESIRE
WILLIAM BUTLER YEATS

The wind blows out of the gates of the day,

The wind blows over the lonely of heart,

And the lonely of heart is withered away,

While the faeries dance in a place apart,

Shaking their milk-white feet in a ring,

Tossing their milk-white arms in the air;

For they hear the wind laugh, and murmur and sing

Of a land where even the old are fair,

And even the wise are merry of tongue;

But I heard a reed of Coolaney say

"When the wind has laughed and murmured and sung,

The lonely of heart is withered away."

VIII
Wise Words

I loafe and invite my soul.
—WALT WHITMAN

AND THE LITTLE MOMENTS,/HUMBLE THOUGH THEY BE,/
MAKE THE MIGHTY AGES/OF ETERNITY.

LIFE IS MOSTLY FROTH AND BUBBLE
ADAM LINDSAY GORDON

Life is mostly froth and bubble,
Two things stand like stone:
Kindness in another's trouble,
Courage in your own.

○

I MAY, I MIGHT, I MUST
MARIANNE MOORE

If you will tell me why the fen
appears impassable, I then
will tell you why I think that I
can get across it if I try.

○

SWEET ARE THE USES OF ADVERSITY
FROM AS YOU LIKE IT, ACT II, SCENE I
WILLIAM SHAKESPEARE

Sweet are the uses of adversity,
Which like the toad, ugly and venomous,
Wears yet a precious jewel in his head.
And this, our life, exempt from public haunt,
Finds tongues in trees, books in the running brooks,
Sermons in stones, and good in everything

THE CELESTIAL SURGEON
ROBERT LOUIS STEVENSON

If I have faltered more or less
In my great task of happiness;
If I have moved among my race
And shown no shining morning face;
If beams from happy human eyes
Have moved me not; if morning skies,
Books, and my food, and summer rain
Knocked on my sullen heart in vain:—
Lord, thy most pointed pleasure take
And stab my spirit broad awake.

JOY OF THE MORNING
EDWIN MARKHAM

I hear you, little bird,
Shouting a-swing above the broken wall.
Shout louder yet: no song can tell it all.
Sing to my soul in the deep, still wood:
'Tis wonderful beyond the wildest word:
I'd tell it, too, if I could.

Oft when the white, still dawn
Lifted the skies and pushed the hills apart,
I've felt it like a glory in my heart—
(The world's mysterious stir)
But had no throat like yours, my bird,
Nor such a listener.

HOPE IS THE THING WITH FEATHERS
EMILY DICKINSON

Hope is the thing with feathers
That perches in the soul,
And sings the tune without the words,
And never stops at all,

And sweetest in the gale is heard;
And sore must be the storm
That could abash the little bird
That kept so many warm.

I've heard it in the chillest land,
And on the strangest sea;
Yet, never, in extremity,
It asked a crumb of me.

○

A NOISELESS PATIENT SPIDER
FROM LEAVES OF GRASS
WALT WHITMAN

A noiseless patient spider,
I mark'd where on a little promontory it stood isolated,
Mark'd how to explore the vacant vast surrounding,
It launch'd forth filament, filament, filament, out of itself,
Ever unreeling them, ever tirelessly speeding them.

And you O my soul where you stand,
Surrounded, detached, in measureless oceans of space,
Ceaselessly musing, venturing, throwing, seeking the spheres to
     connect them,
Till the bridge you will need be form'd, till the ductile anchor hold,
Till the gossamer thread you fling catch somewhere, O my soul.

I CELEBRATE MYSELF, AND SING MYSELF

FROM "SONG OF MYSELF"
WALT WHITMAN

I

I celebrate myself, and sing myself,
And what I shall assume, you shall assume;
For every atom belonging to me as good belongs to you.
I loafe and invite my soul,
I lean and loafe at my ease observing a spear of summer grass.

. . . .

31

I believe a leaf of grass is no less than the journey-work of the stars,
And the pismire is equally perfect, and a grain of sand, and the egg
    of the wren,
And the tree-toad is a chef-d'oeuvre for the highest,
And the running blackberry would adorn the parlors of heaven,
And the narrowest hinge in my hand puts to scorn all machinery,
And the cow crunching with depress'd head surpasses any statue,
And a mouse is miracle enough to stagger sextillions of infidels.

○

ABOU BEN ADHEM

JAMES HENRY LEIGH HUNT

Abou Ben Adhem (may his tribe increase!)
Awoke one night from a deep dream of peace,
And saw, within the moonlight in his room,
  Making it rich, and like a lily in bloom,
An angel writing in a book of gold:—
  Exceeding peace had made Ben Adhem bold,
And to the Presence in the room he said,
"What writest thou?"—The vision raised its head,
  And with a look made of all sweet accord,
Answered, "The names of those who love the Lord."

"And is mine one?" said Abou. "Nay, not so,"
  Replied the angel. Abou spoke more low,
  But cheerily still, and said, "I pray thee, then,
  Write me as one that loves his fellow men."

The angel wrote, and vanished. The next night
  It came again with a great wakening light,
  And showed the names whom love of God had blessed,
  And lo! Ben Adhem's name led all the rest.

◎

THE FAITHFUL SERVANTS OF THE BENEFICENT
FROM THE KORAN 25:63

The faithful servants of the beneficent (God) are they who walk
upon the earth modestly, and when the foolish ones address them,
they say, "Peace."

◎

HE THAT IS SLOW TO ANGER
FROM THE KING JAMES VERSION OF THE BIBLE, PROVERBS 14:32

He that is slow to anger is better than the mighty;
  And he that ruleth his spirit than he that taketh a city.

FROM AUGURIES OF INNOCENCE
WILLIAM BLAKE

Man was made for Joy & Woe;
And when this we rightly know
Thro' the World we safely go.
Joy & Woe are woven fine,
A Clothing for the Soul divine;
Under every grief & pine
Runs a joy with silken twine.

◎

AGAINST IDLENESS AND MISCHIEF
ISAAC WATTS

How doth the little busy bee
  Improve each shining hour
And gather honey all the day
  From every opening flower

How skillfully she builds her cell!
  How neat she spreads the wax!
And labors hard to store it well
  With the sweet food she makes.

In works of labor or of skill
  I would be busy too;
For Satan finds some mischief still
  For idle hands to do!

In books, or work, or healthful play,
  Let my first years be passed,
That I may give for every day
  Some good account at last.

LITTLE THINGS

JULIA A. CARNEY

Little drops of water,
   Little grains of sand,
Make the mighty ocean
   And the beauteous land.

And the little moments,
   Humble though they be,
Make the mighty ages
   Of eternity.

So our little errors
   Lead the soul away,
From the paths of virtue
   Into sin to stray.

Little deeds of kindness,
   Little words of love,
Make our earth an Eden,
   Like the heaven above.

THE BLIND MEN AND THE ELEPHANT

JOHN GODFREY SAXE

It was six men of Hindostan,
To learning much inclined,
Who went to see the elephant,
(Though all of them were blind);
That each by observation
Might satisfy his mind.

The first approached the elephant,
And happening to fall
Against his broad and sturdy side,
At once began to bawl,
"Bless me, it seems the elephant
Is very like a wall."

The second, feeling of his tusk,
Cried, "Ho! what have we here
So very round and smooth and sharp?
To me 'tis mighty clear
This wonder of an elephant
Is very like a spear."

The third approached the animal,
And happening to take
The squirming trunk within his hands,
Then boldly up and spake;
"I see," quoth he, "the elephant
Is very like a snake."

The fourth stretched out his eager hand
And felt about the knee,
"What most this mighty beast is like
Is mighty plain," quoth he;
"'Tis clear enough the elephant
Is very like a tree."

The fifth who chanced to touch the ear
Said, "Even the blindest man
Can tell what this resembles most;
Deny the fact who can,
The marvel of an elephant
Is very like a fan."

The sixth no sooner had begun
About the beast to grope
Than, seizing on the swinging tail
That fell within his scope,
"I see," cried he, "the elephant
Is very like a rope."

And so these men of Hindostan
Disputed loud and long,
Each of his own opinion
Exceeding stiff and strong,
Though each was partly in the right,
And all were in the wrong!

○

FOR WANT OF A NAIL

For want of a nail
The shoe was lost.
For want of the shoe
The horse was lost.
For want of the horse
The rider was lost.
For want of the rider
The battle was lost.
For want of the battle
The kingdom was lost;
And all for the want
Of a horseshoe nail.

THE SLUGGARD
ISAAC WATTS

'Tis the voice of a sluggard; I hear him complain,
"You have waked me too soon, I must slumber again;"
As the door on its hinges, so he on his bed,
Turns his sides and his shoulders, and his heavy head.

"A little more sleep, and a little more slumber;"
Thus he wastes half his days, and his hours without number;
And when he gets up, he sits folding his hands,
Or walks about sauntering, or trifling he stands;

I passed by his garden, and saw the wild brier,
The thorn and the thistle grow broader and higher;
The clothes that hang on him are turning to rags;
And his money still wastes till he starves or he begs.

I made him a visit still hoping to find
He had took better care for improving his mind;
He told me his dreams, talk'd of eating and drinking,
But he scarce reads his Bible, and never loves thinking.

Said I then to my heart, "Here's a lesson for me;
That man's but a picture of what I might be.
But thanks to my friends for their care in my breeding,
Who taught me betimes to love working and reading."

○

THE THINGS, GOOD LORD, THAT WE PRAY FOR
SAINT THOMAS MORE

The things, good Lord, that we pray for, give
us the grace to labor for.

GREEDY RICHARD

JANE TAYLOR

"I think I want some pies this morning,"
Said Dick, stretching himself and yawning;
So down he threw his slate and books,
And sauntered to the pastry-cook's.

And there he cast his greedy eyes,
Round on the jellies and the pies,
So to select, with anxious care,
The very nicest that was there.

At last the point was thus decided:
As his opinion was divided
'Twixt pie and jelly, he was loath
Either to leave, so took them both.

Now Richard never could be pleased
To stop when hunger was appeased,
But he'd go on to eat and stuff,
Long after he had had enough.

"I shan't take any more," said Dick,
"Dear me, I feel extremely sick:
I cannot eat this other bit;
I wish I had not tasted it."

Then slowly rising from his seat,
He threw his cheesecake in the street,
And left the tempting pastry-cook's,
With very discontented looks.

Just then a man with wooden leg
Met Dick, and held his hat to beg;
And while he told his mournful case,
Looked at him with imploring face.

Dick, wishing to relieve his pain,
His pocket searched, but searched in vain,
And so at last he did declare,
He had not got a farthing there.

The beggar turned, with face of grief,
And look of patient unbelief,
While Richard, now completely tamed,
Felt inconceivably ashamed.

"I wish," said he (but wishing's vain),
"I had my money back again,
And had not spent my last, to pay
For what I only threw away.

"Another time I'll take advice,
And not buy things because they're nice;
But rather save my little store
To give poor folks, who want it more."

○

SHIELD YOURSELVES AGAINST HELL FIRE
FROM "TEACHINGS OF THE PROPHET MUHAMMAD"
AL-BUKHARI

Adi Bin Hatim says,
"Shield yourselves against hell fire even if it be only half a date
given in charity; and one who cannot afford that much should
at least speak nicely."

THE ADVENTURES OF ISABEL

OGDEN NASH

Isabel met an enormous bear,
Isabel, Isabel, didn't care;
The bear was hungry, the bear was ravenous,
The bear's big mouth was cruel and cavernous.
The bear said, Isabel, glad to meet you,
How do, Isabel, now I'll eat you!
Isabel, Isabel, didn't worry.
Isabel didn't scream or scurry.
She washed her hands and she straightened her hair up.
Then Isabel quietly ate the bear up.
Once in a night as black as pitch
Isabel met a wicked old witch.
the witch's face was cross and wrinkled,
The witch's gums with teeth were sprinkled.
Ho, ho, Isabel! the old witch crowed,
I'll turn you into an ugly toad!
Isabel, Isabel, didn't worry,
Isabel didn't scream or scurry.
She showed no rage and she showed no rancor,
But she turned the witch into milk and drank her.
Isabel met a hideous giant,
Isabel continued self reliant.
The giant was hairy, the giant was horrid,
He had one eye in the middle of his forhead.
Good morning, Isabel, the giant said,
I'll grind your bones to make my bread.
Isabel, Isabel, didn't worry,
Isabel didn't scream or scurry.
She nibled the zwieback that she always fed off,
And when it was gone, she cut the giant's head off.

Isabel met a troublesome doctor,
He punched and he poked till he really shocked her.
The doctor's talk was of coughs and chills
And the doctor's satchel bulged with pills.
The doctor said unto Isabel,
Swallow this, it will make you well.
Isabel, Isabel, didn't worry,
Isabel didn't scream or scurry.
She took those pills from the pill concocter,
And Isabel calmly cured the doctor.

◎

THE DRUM
NIKKI GIOVANNI

daddy says the world is
a drum tight and hard
and i told him
i'm gonna beat
out my own rhythm

◎

INVICTUS
WILLIAM ERNEST HENLEY

Out of the night that covers me,
    Black as the Pit from pole to pole,
I thank whatever gods may be
    For my unconquerable soul.

In the fell clutch of circumstance
    I have not winced nor cried aloud.
Under the bludgeonings of chance
    My head is bloody, but unbowed.

Beyond this place of wrath and tears
    Looms but the horror of the shade,
And yet the menace of the years
    Finds, and shall find me, unafraid.

It matters not how strait the gate,
    How charged with punishments the scroll,
I am the master of my fate:
    I am the captain of my soul.

◎

IF

RUDYARD KIPLING

If you can keep your head when all about you
Are losing theirs and blaming it on you;
If you can trust yourself when all men doubt you,
But make allowance for their doubting too:
If you can wait and not be tired by waiting,
Or, being lied about, don't deal in lies,
Or being hated don't give way to hating,
And yet don't look too good, nor talk too wise;

If you can dream—and not make dreams your master;
If you can think—and not make thoughts your aim,
If you can meet with Triumph and Disaster
And treat those two impostors just the same;
If you can bear to hear the truth you've spoken
Twisted by knaves to make a trap for fools,
Or watch the things you gave your life to, broken,
And stoop and build' em up with worn-out tools;

If you can make one heap of all your winnings
And risk it on one turn of pitch-and-toss,
And lose, and start again at your beginnings,
And never breathe a word about your loss:
If you can force your heart and nerve and sinew
To serve your turn long after they are gone,
And so hold on when there is nothing in you
Except the Will which says to them: "Hold on!"

If you can talk with crowds and keep your virtue,
Or walk with Kings—nor lose the common touch,
If neither foes nor loving friends can hurt you,
If all men count with you, but none too much:
If you can fill the unforgiving minute
With sixty seconds' worth of distance run,
Yours is the Earth and everything that's in it,
And—which is more—you'll be a Man, my son!

IX
My Country

My country, 'Tis of Thee,
Sweet land of liberty,
Of thee I sing!

—*SAMUEL FRANCIS SMITH*

...THE GREAT TASK REMAINING BEFORE US...

YANKEE DOODLE

Yankee Doodle went to town
A-riding on a pony
Stuck a feather in his cap
And called it macaroni.

Chorus
Yankee Doodle, keep it up
Yankee Doodle dandy
Mind the music and the step
And with the girls be handy.

Father and I went down to camp
Along with Cap'n Goodwin
And there we saw the men and boys
As thick as hasty pudding.

Chorus

There was Captain Washington
Upon a slapping stallion
A-giving orders to his men
I guess there was a million.

Chorus

And there we see a thousand men,
As rich as Squire David;
And what they wasted ev'ry day,
I wish it could be saved.

Chorus

And there I see a swamping gun,
Large as a log of maple,
Upon a deuced little cart,
A load for father's cattle.

Chorus

And every time they shoot it off,
It takes a horn of powder,
And makes a noise like father's gun,
Only a nation louder.

Chorus

We saw a little barrel, too,
The heads were made of leather;
They knocked upon it with little clubs,
And called the folks together.

Chorus

And there they'd fife away like fun,
And play on cornstalk fiddles,
And some had ribbons red as blood,
All bound around their middles.

Chorus

The troopers, too, would gallop up
And fire right in our faces;
It scared me almost to death
To see them run such races.

Chorus

Yankee Doodle went to town
A-riding on a pony
Stuck a feather in his cap
And called it macaroni.

Yankee Doodle, keep it up
Yankee Doodle dandy
Mind the music and the step
And with the girls be handy.

THE MIDNIGHT RIDE OF PAUL REVERE

HENRY WADSWORTH LONGFELLOW

Listen, my children, and you shall hear
Of the midnight ride of Paul Revere,
On the eighteenth of April, in Seventy-five;
Hardly a man is now alive
Who remembers that famous day and year.

He said to his friend, "If the British march
By land or sea from the town tonight,
Hang a lantern aloft in the belfry arch
Of the North Church tower as a signal light—
One, if by land, and two, if by sea;
And I on the opposite shore will be,
Ready to ride and spread the alarm
Through every Middlesex village and farm,
For the country folk to be up and to arm."

The he said, "Good night!" and with muffled oar
Silently rowed to the Charlestown shore,
Just as the moon rose over the bay,
Where swinging wide at her moorings lay
The *Somerset,* British man-of-war;
A phantom ship, with each mast and spar
Across the moon like a prison bar,
And a huge black hulk, that was magnified
By its own reflection in the tide.

Meanwhile, his friend, through alley and street,
Wanders and watches, with eager ears,
Till in the silence around him he hears
The muster of men at the barrack door,
And the measured tread of the grenadiers,
Marching down to their boats on the shore.

Then he climbed to the tower of the Old North Church,
By the wooden stairs, with stealthy tread,
To the belfry-chamber overhead,

And startled the pigeons from their perch
On the somber rafters, that round him made
Masses and moving shapes of shade—
By the trembling ladder, steep and tall,
To the highest window in the wall,
Where he paused to listen and look down
A moment on the roofs of the town,
And the moonlight flowing over all.

Beneath in the churchyard, lay the dead,
In their night-encampment on the hill,
Wrapped in silence so deep and still
That he could hear, like a sentinel's tread,
The watchful night-wind, as it went
Creeping along from tent to tent,
And seeming to whisper, "All is well!"
A moment only he feels the spell
Of the place and the hour, and the secret dread
Of the lonely belfry and the dead;
For suddenly all his thoughts are bent
On a shadowy something far away,
Where the river widens to meet the bay—
A line of black that bends and floats
On the rising tide, like a bridge of boats.

Meanwhile, impatient to mount and ride,
Booted and spurred, with a heavy stride
On the opposite shore walked Paul Revere.
Now he patted his horse's side,
Now gazed at the landscape far and near,
Then, impetuous, stamped the earth,
And turned and tightened his saddle girth;
But mostly he watched with eager search
The belfry tower of the Old North Church,
As it rose above the graves on the hill,
Lonely and spectral and somber and still.

And lo! as he looks, on the belfry's height
A glimmer, and then a gleam of light!
He springs to the saddle, the bridle he turns,
But lingers and gazes, till full on his sight
A second lamp in the belfry burns!

A hurry of hoofs in a village street,
A shape in the moonlight, a bulk in the dark,
And beneath, from the pebbles, in passing, a spark
Struck out by a steed flying fearless and fleet:
That was all! And yet, through the gloom and the light,
The fate of a nation was riding that night;
And the spark struck out by that steed, in his flight,
Kindled the land into flame with its heat.

He has left the village and mounted the steep,
And beneath him, tranquil and broad and deep,
Is the Mystic, meeting the ocean tides;
And under the alders that skirt its edge,
Now soft on the sand, now loud on the ledge,
Is heard the tramp of his steed as he rides.

It was twelve by the village clock,
When he crossed the bridge into Medford town.
He heard the crowing of the cock,
And the barking of the farmer's dog,
And felt the damp of the river fog,
That rises after the sun goes down.
It was one by the village clock,
When he galloped into Lexington.
He saw the gilded weathercock
Swim in the moonlight as he passed,
And the meeting-house window, blank and bare,
Gaze at him with a spectral glare,
As if they already stood aghast
At the bloody work they would look upon.

It was two by the village clock,
When he came to the bridge in Concord town.
He heard the bleating of the flock,
And the twitter of birds among the trees,
And felt the breath of the morning breeze
Blowing over the meadows brown.
And one was safe and asleep in his bed
Who at the bridge would be first to fall,
Who that day would be lying dead,
Pierced by a British musket-ball.

You know the rest. In the books you have read
How the British Regulars fired and fled—
How the farmers gave them ball for ball,
From behind each fence and farmyard wall,
Chasing the red-coats down the lane,
Then crossing the fields to emerge again
Under the trees at the turn of the road,
And only pausing to fire and load.

So through the night rode Paul Revere;
And so through the night went his cry of alarm
To every Middlesex village and farm—
A cry of defiance and not of fear,
A voice in the darkness, a knock at the door,
And a word that shall echo for evermore!
For, borne on the night-wind of the Past,
Through all our history, to the last,
In the hour of darkness and peril and need,
The people will awaken and listen to hear
The hurrying hoof-beats of that steed,
And the midnight message of Paul Revere.

Every part of this soil is sacred in the estimation of my people.
Every hillside, every valley, every plain and grove, has been hallowed
by some sad or happy event in days long vanished. Even the rocks,
which seem to be dumb and dead as they swelter in the sun along
the silent shore, thrill with memories of stirring events connected
with the lives of my people, and the very dust upon which you
now stand responds more lovingly to their footsteps than yours,
because it is rich with the blood of our ancestors, and our bare feet
are conscious of the sympathetic touch. Our departed braves, fond
mothers, glad, happy hearted maidens, and even the little children
who lived here and rejoiced here for a brief season, will love these
somber solitudes and at eventide they greet shadowy returning
spirits. And when the last Red Man shall have perished, and the
memory of my tribe shall have become a myth among the White
Men, these shores will swarm with the invisible dead of my tribe,
and when your children's children think themselves alone in the
field, the store, the shop, upon the highway, or in the silence of the
pathless woods, they will not be alone. In all the earth there is no
place dedicated to solitude. At night when the streets of your cities
and villages are silent and you think them deserted, they will throng
with the returning hosts that once filled them and still love this
beautiful land. The White Man will never be alone.

I Hear America Singing

FROM LEAVES OF GRASS
WALT WHITMAN

I hear America singing, the varied carols I hear;
Those of mechanics—each one singing his, as it should be, blithe
 and strong;
The carpenter singing his, as he measures his plank or beam,
The mason singing his, as he makes ready for work, or leaves off work;
The boatman singing what belongs to him in his boat—the
 deckhand singing on the steamboat deck;
The shoemaker singing as he sits on his bench—the hatter singing as
 he stands;
The wood-cutter's song—the ploughboy's, on his way in the morning,
 or at the noon intermission, or at sundown;
The delicious singing of the mother—or of the young wife at work—
 or of the girl sewing or washing—Each singing what belongs to her,
 and to none else;
The day what belongs to the day—At night, the party of young
 fellows, robust, friendly,
Singing, with open mouths, their strong melodious songs.

BATTLE-HYMN OF THE REPUBLIC

JULIA WARD HOWE

Mine eyes have seen the glory of the coming of the Lord:
He is trampling out the vintage where the grapes of wrath are
   stored;
He hath loosed the fateful lightning of his terrible swift sword:
        His truth is marching on.

I have seen Him in the watch-fires of a hundred circling camps:
They have builded Him an altar in the evening dews and damps;
I can read his righteous sentence by the dim and flaring lamps.
        His day is marching on.

He has sounded forth the trumpet that shall never call retreat;
He is sifting out the hearts of men before his judgment seat;
Oh! be swift, my soul, to answer Him! be jubilant, my feet!
        Our God is marching on.

In the beauty of the lilies Christ was born across the sea,
With a glory in his bosom that transfigures you and me:
As He died to make men holy, let us die to make men free,
        While God is marching on.

THE GETTYSBURG ADDRESS

DELIVERED AT GETTYSBURG, PENNSYLVANIA
NOVEMBER 19, 1863
ABRAHAM LINCOLN

Fourscore and seven years ago our fathers brought forth on
this continent a new nation, conceived in liberty, and dedicated
to the proposition that all men are created equal.

Now we are engaged in a great civil war, testing whether that nation,
or any nation so conceived and so dedicated, can long endure. We
are met on a great battlefield of that war. We have come to dedicate
a portion of that field as a final resting-place for those who here
gave their lives that that nation might live. It is altogether fitting
and proper that we should do this.

But in a larger sense, we cannot dedicate, we cannot consecrate,
we cannot hallow this ground. The brave men, living and dead,
who struggled here, have consecrated it far above our poor power
to add or detract. The world will little note, nor long remember,
what we say here; but it can never forget what they did here. It is
for us, the living, rather, to be dedicated here to the unfinished
work which they who fought here have thus far so nobly advanced.
It is rather for us to be here dedicated to the great task remaining
before us, that from these honored dead we take increased
devotion to that cause for which they gave the last full measure
of devotion; that we here highly resolve that these dead shall not
have died in vain; that this nation, under God, shall have a new
birth of freedom; and that government of the people, by the
people, for the people, shall not perish from the earth.

O Captain! My Captain!

WALT WHITMAN

O Captain! my Captain! our fearful trip is done;
The ship has weather'd every rack, the prize we sought is won;
The port is near, the bells I hear, the people all exulting,
While follow eyes the steady keel, the vessel grim and daring:
But O heart! heart! heart!
O the bleeding drops of red,
Where on the deck my Captain lies,
Fallen cold and dead.

O Captain! my Captain! rise up and hear the bells;
Rise up—for you the flag is flung—for you the bugle trills;
For you bouquets and ribbon'd wreaths—for you the shores a-crowding;
For you they call, the swaying mass, their eager faces turning;
Here Captain! dear father!
This arm beneath your head;
It is some dream that on the deck,
You've fallen cold and dead.

My Captain does not answer, his lips are pale and still;
My father does not feel my arm, he has no pulse nor will;
The ship is anchor'd safe and sound, its voyage closed and done;
From fearful trip, the victor ship, comes in with object won;
Exult, O shores, and ring, O bells!
But I, with mournful tread,
Walk the deck my Captain lies,
Fallen cold and dead.

FAREWELL ADDRESS

FROM THE FAREWELL ADDRESS OF CHIEF PLENTY COUPS OF THE CROW PEOPLE GIVEN IN 1909 AT THE LITTLE BIGHORN COUNCIL GROUNDS IN MONTANA

The Ground on which we stand is sacred ground.
It is the dust and blood of our ancestors. On these
plains, the Great White Father at Washington
sent his soldiers armed with long knives and rifles
to slay the Indian. Many of them sleep
on yonder hill, where Pahaska—White Chief
of the Long Hair[1]—so bravely
fought and fell. A few more passing suns
will see us here no more. And our dust and bones
will mingle with these same prairies.

I see as in a vision the dying spark
of our council fires, the ashes cold and white.
I see no longer the curling smoke rising
from our lodge poles. I hear no longer the songs
of the women as they prepare the meal.
The antelope have gone; the buffalo wallows
are empty. Only the wail of the coyote is heard.

The white man's medicine is stronger than ours;
his iron horse rushes over the buffalo trail.
He talks to us through his "whispering spirit."[2]
We are like birds with a broken wing.
My heart is cold within me.
My eyes are growing dim. I am old ...

———————

[1] General Custer
[2] The telephone

THE FLOWER-FED BUFFALOES

VACHEL LINDSAY

The flower-fed buffaloes of the spring
In the days of long ago,
Ranged where the locomotives sing
And the prairie flowers lie low;
The tossing, blooming, perfumed grass
Is swept away by wheat,
Wheels and wheels and wheels spin by
In the spring that still is sweet.
But the flower-fed buffaloes of the spring
Left us long ago.

○

THE NEW COLOSSUS

EMMA LAZARUS

Not like the brazen giant of Greek fame
With conquering limbs astride from land to land;
Here at our sea-washed, sunset gates shall stand
A mighty woman with a torch, whose flame
Is the imprisoned lightning, and her name
Mother of Exiles. From her beacon-hand
Glows world-wide welcome; her mild eyes command
The air-bridged harbor that twin cities frame,
"Keep, ancient lands, your storied pomp!" cries she
With silent lips. "Give me your tired, your poor,
Your huddled masses yearning to breathe free,
The wretched refuse of your teeming shore,
Send these, the homeless, tempest-tossed to me,
I lift my lamp beside the golden door!"

I, TOO, SING AMERICA

LANGSTON HUGHES

I, too, sing America.

I am the darker brother.
They send me to eat in the kitchen
When company comes,
But I laugh,
And eat well,
And grow strong.

Tomorrow,
I'll be at the table
When company comes.
Nobody'll dare
Say to me,
"Eat in the kitchen,"
Then.

Besides,
They'll see how beautiful I am
And be ashamed—

I, too, am America.

FROM I HAVE A DREAM

MARTIN LUTHER KING, JR.

So I say to you, my friends, that even though we must face the difficulties of today and tomorrow, I still have a dream. It is a dream deeply rooted in the American dream that one day this nation will rise up and live out the true meaning of its creed—we hold these truths to be self evident, that all men are created equal.

. . . .

I have a dream that one day on the red hills of Georgia, sons of former slaves and sons of former slave-owners will be able to sit down together at the table of brotherhood.

. . . .

I have a dream my four little children will one day live in a nation where they will not be judged by the color of their skin but by content of their character. I have a dream today!

. . . .

I have a dream that one day every valley shall be exalted, every hill and mountain shall be made low, the rough places shall be made plain, and the crooked places shall be made straight and the glory of the Lord will be revealed and all flesh shall see it together.

. . . .

With this faith we will be able to work together, to pray together, to struggle together, to go to jail together, to stand up for freedom together, knowing that we will be free one day. This will be the day when all God's children will be able to sing with new meaning— "my country 'tis of thee; sweet land of liberty; of thee I sing; land where my fathers died, land of the pilgrim's pride; from every mountain side, let freedom ring"—and if America is to be a great nation, this must become true.

So let freedom ring from the prodigious hilltops of New Hampshire.

Let freedom ring from the mighty mountains of New York.

Let freedom ring from the heightening Alleghenies of Pennsylvania.

Let freedom ring from the snow-capped Rockies of Colorado.

Let freedom ring from the curvaceous slopes of California.

But not only that.

Let freedom ring from Stone Mountain of Georgia.

Let freedom ring from Lookout Mountain of Tennessee.

Let freedom ring from every hill and molehill of Mississippi, from every mountainside, let freedom ring.

And when we allow freedom to ring, when we let it ring from every village and hamlet, from every state and city, we will be able to speed up that day when all of God's children—black men and white men, Jews and Gentiles, Catholics and Protestants—will be able to join hands and to sing in the words of the old Negro spiritual. "Free at last, free at last; thank God Almighty, we are free at last."

◎

NIGHT GAME
LILLIAN MORRISON

At first I thought it was the moon
gliding down with one
shining arm outstretched
carrying something dark.
Then I realized
it was the Statue of Liberty
arcing slowly through the sky
with a baseball glove on her
uplifted hand. She was saying,
"Umpire, you blind burglar,
You can't throw me out of the game."

Pastoral I [First Version]

WILLIAM CARLOS WILLIAMS

When I was younger
it was plain to me
I must make something of myself.
Older now
I walk back streets
admiring the houses
of the very poor:
roof out of line with sides
the yards cluttered
with old chicken wire, ashes,
furniture gone wrong;
the fences and outhouses
built of barrel-staves
and parts of boxes, all,
if I am fortunate,
smeared a bluish green
that properly weathered
pleases me best
of all colors.

       No one
will believe this
of vast import to the nation.

INCIDENT

FOR ERIC WALROND
COUNTEE CULLEN

Once riding in old Baltimore,
    Heart-filled, head-filled with glee,
I saw a Baltimorean
    Keep looking straight at me.

Now I was eight and very small,
    And he was no whit bigger,
And so I smiled, but he poked out
    His tongue, and called me, "Nigger."

I saw the whole of Baltimore
    From May until December;
Of all the things that happened there
    That's all that I remember.

○

MEXICO CITY BLUES (221ST CHORUS)

JACK KEROUAC

Old Man Mose
Early American Jazz pianist
Had a grandson
Called Deadbelly.
Old Man Mose walloped
    the rollickin keyport
    Wahoo wildhouse Piany
    with monkies in his hair
    drooling spaghetti, beer
    and beans, with a cigar
    mashed in his countenance
    of gleaming happiness
    the furtive madman
    of old sane times.

Deadbelly dont hide it—
    Lead killed Leadbelly—
Deadbelly admit
    Deadbelly modern cat
Cool—Deadbelly, Man,
Craziest.
        Old Man Mose is Dead
        But Deadbelly get Ahead
        Ha ha ha

◎

TALKING DUST BOWL BLUES
WOODY GUTHRIE

Back in Nineteen Twenty-Seven,
I had a little farm and I called that heaven.
Well, price was up and the rain come down,
And I hauled my crops all into town—
I got the money, bought clothes and groceries,
Fed the kids, and raised a family.

Rain quit and the wind got high,
And the black ol' dust storm filled the sky.
And I swapped my farm for a Ford machine,
And I poured it full of this gas-i-line—
And I started, rockin' an' a-rollin',
Over the mountains, out towards the old Peach Bowl.

Way up yonder on a mountain road,
I had a hot motor and a heavy load,
I's a-goin' pretty fast, there wasn't even stoppin',
A-bouncin' up and down, like popcorn poppin'—
Had a breakdown, sort of a nervous bustdown of some kind,
There was a feller there, a mechanic feller,
Said it was en-gine trouble.

Way up yonder on a mountain curve,
It's way up yonder in the piney wood,
An' I give that rollin' Ford a shove,
An' I's a-gonna coast as far as I could—
Commence coastin', pickin' up speed,
Was a hairpin turn, I didn't make it.

Man alive, I'm a-tellin' you,
The fiddles and the guitars really flew.
That Ford took off like a flying squirrel
An' it flew halfway around the world—
Scattered wives and childrens
All over the side of that mountain.

We got out to the West Coast broke,
So dad-gum hungry I thought I'd croak,
An' I bummed up a spud or two,
An' my wife fixed up a tater stew—
We poured the kids full of it,
Mighty thin stew, though,
You could read a magazine right through it.
Always have figured
That if it'd been just a little bit thinner,
Some of these here politicians
Coulda seen through it.

THIS LAND IS YOUR LAND

WOODY GUTHRIE

This land is your land,
    This land is my land,
From California
    to the New York island;
From the redwood forest
    to the Gulf Stream waters,
This land was made for you and me.

As I was walking
    that ribbon of highway,
I saw above me
    that endless skyway:
I saw below me
    that golden valley:
This land was made for you and me.

I've roamed and rambled,
    and I followed my footsteps
To the sparkling sands of
    her diamond deserts;
And all around me
    a voice was sounding:
This land was made for you and me.

When the sun came shining,
    and I was strolling,
And the wheat fields waving
    and the dust clouds rolling,
As the fog was lifting
    a voice was chanting:
This land was made for you and me.

In the shadow of the steeple
    I saw my people,
By the relief office
    I seen my people;
As they stood there hungry,
    I stood there asking
Is this land made for you and me?

Nobody living
    can ever stop me,
As I go walking
    that freedom highway;
Nobody living
    can ever make me turn back,
This land was made for you and me.

"WHO ARE YOU REALLY, WANDERER?"

X
Travel

I should like to rise and go
Where the golden apples grow
—ROBERT LOUIS STEVENSON

THE WANDERER'S SONG
TRADITIONAL SOUTH AFRICAN SONG

In the shade I lie and ponder
As the sun's rays beat out yonder—
My one wish is that I
May wander the world 'til I die.

I will seek valleys enchanted,
I will find lakes that are haunted.
Heat, cold, wind, drowning rain—
A wanderer I will remain.

○

FROM TRAVEL
ROBERT LOUIS STEVENSON

I should like to rise and go
Where the golden apples grow;
Where below another sky
Parrot Islands anchored lie,
. . . .

Where in sunshine reaching out
Eastern cities, miles about,
Are with mosque and minaret
Among sandy gardens set,
And the rich goods from near and far
Hang for sale in the bazaar;
Where the Great Wall round China goes,
And on one side the desert blows,
And with bell and voice and drum,
Cities on the other hum;
Where are forests, hot as fire,
Wide as England, tall as a spire,
. . . .

Where the knotty crocodile
Lies and blinks in the Nile,
And the red flamingo flies
Hunting fish before his eyes;
. . . .

Where in jungles, near and far,
Man-devouring tigers are,
Lying close and giving ear
Lest the hunt be drawing near,
Or a comer-by be seen
Swinging in a palanquin;
Where among the desert sands
Some deserted city stands,
All its children, sweep and prince,
Grown to manhood ages since,
Not a foot in street or house,
Not a stir of child or mouse,
And when kindly falls the night,
In all the town no spark of light.
There I'll come when I'm a man
With a camel caravan;
Light a fire in the gloom
Of some dusty dining room;
See the pictures on the walls,
Heroes, fights, and festivals;
And in a corner find the toys
Of the old Egyptian boys.

SAILOR JOHN

DAVID MCCORD

Young Stephen has a young friend John
Who in his years is getting on.
He's getting on for six, I think,
Or seven. Yes, he's on the brink
Of seven, which is pretty old
Unless you're eight or nine all told.
But anyhow, John has a notion
That he would like to sail the ocean.
He has the notion, understand,
But not the ocean—just the land.
John hasn't any boat as yet,
Although his feet are often wet:
They're wet today because of rain.
Quite right—he can't go out again
Unless he finds some other shoes.
John has a notion he will choose
To stay inside and shut the door
And lie right down upon the floor
And think about the ocean, how
It's not available just now;
And think about the kinds of boat
He doesn't have that wouldn't float.

○

FROM FRIENDS

LOU LAHR

Timmy and Tommy and Toby and me
Went round the world, the round world to see;
And what we like best, as I can recall
Was just being together and all.

We went to England, to Spain and to France;
To China and India to see the snakes dance.
And what liked we best on the great China wall?
O, just being together and all.

On then to Russia where a great Russian bear
Caught Toby so Tom and I pulled out his hair!
We just *bear*ly escaped! what a fix we were in!
But we stuck together through thick and thin.

Homesickness got Tim. He cried all one night.
And we all sniffled some, but we never did fight.

. . . .

We climbed the high mountains and slid down again.
We sailed the high seas, then dove deep into them.
We found sunken treasures, we found snow-man tracks,
We gave each other the shirts off our backs!

We traveled by land and by sea and by air
From our many adventures we learned how to share,
To roll with the punches and hold ourselves tall,
Just being together and all!

Well, we wearied at last of adventures afar
And longed to go home to our Ma and our Pa.
So we bade a farewell to the lands of our dreams,
Raised top-sail, weighed anchor and took to the foam.

But a big storm came up as we rounded The Horn;
Our vessel capsized and I thought we were gone.
The sky was so dark and the sea was so deep,
I sang "Rock of Ages" to calm my heart's beat.

Then a bold flash of lightning illumined the sky
And spread out on the water, enough to see by.
At first I saw nothing, no boat and no one,
Just me by myself, all alone.

Then I saw my friend Toby pop up from the sea
And Toby saw Timmy and Timmy saw me;
So none of us drownded and home we did haul,
Just pulling together and all!

Then "What liked you best," the people exclaimed
"Of the seas that you sailed and the mountains you climbed,
Of the deserts you traversed and stars you observed
As thick in the sky as gooseberry preserves?"

Well, we pondered the question, we pondered it hard
And wrote out these verses, like Shakespeare the bard,
That what we liked best in all the wide world
Was just being together and all!

○

FROM THE JUMBLIES
EDWARD LEAR

I
They went to sea in a Sieve, they did,
    In a Sieve they went to sea:
In spite of all their friends could say,
On a winter's morn, on a stormy day,
    In a Sieve they went to sea!
And when the Sieve turned round and round,
And everyone cried, "You all be drowned!"
They called aloud, "Our Sieve ain't big,
But we don't care a button! We don't care a fig!
    In a Sieve we'll go to sea!"
        Far and few, far and few,
            Are the lands where the Jumblies live;
            Their heads are green, and their hands are blue,
                And they went to sea in a Sieve.

. . . .

III

The water it soon came in, it did,
    The water it soon came in;
So to keep them dry, they wrapped their feet
In a pinky paper all folded neat,
    And they fastened it down with a pin.
And they passed the night in a crockery-jar,
And each of them said, "How wise we are,"
Though the sky be dark, and the voyage be long,
Yet we never can think we were rash or wrong,
While round in our Sieve we spin!"
    Far and few, far and few,
        Are the lands where the Jumblies live;
    Their heads are green, and their hands are blue,
        And they went to sea in a Sieve.

. . . .

V

They sailed to the Western Sea, they did,
    To a land all covered with trees,
And they bought an Owl, and a useful Cart,
And a pound of Rice, and a Cranberry Tart,
    And a hive of silvery bees.
And they bought a pig, and some green Jack-daws,
And a lovely Monkey with lollypop paws,
And forty bottle of Ring-Bo-Ree,
And no end of Stilton cheese.
    Far and few, far and few,
        Are the lands where the Jumblies live;
    Their heads are green, and their hands are blue,
        And they went to sea in a Sieve.

VI

And in twenty years they all came back,
    In twenty years or more,
And everyone said, "How tall they've grown!
For they've been to the Lakes, and the Torrible Zone,
    And the hills of Chankly Bore";
And they drank their health, and gave them a feast
Of dumplings made of beautiful yeast;
And everyone said, "If we only live,
We too will go to sea in a Sieve,—
To the hills of Chankly Bore!"
    Far and few, far and few,
      Are the lands where the Jumblies live;
     Their heads are green, and their hands are blue,
      And they went to sea in a Sieve.

◎

THE LAND OF STORY-BOOKS

ROBERT LOUIS STEVENSON

At evening when the lamp is lit,
Around the fire my parents sit;
They sit at home and talk and sing,
And do not play at anything.

Now, with my little gun, I crawl
All in the dark along the wall,
And follow round the forest track
Away behind the sofa back.

There, in the night, where none can spy,
All in my hunter's camp I lie,
And play at books that I have read
Till it is time to go to bed.

These are the hills, these are the woods,
These are my starry solitudes;
And there the river by whose brink
The roaring lions come to drink.

I see the others far away
As if in firelit camp they lay,
And I, like to an Indian scout,
Around their party prowled about.

So, when my nurse comes in for me,
Home I return across the sea,
And go to bed with backward looks
At my dear Land of Story Books.

◎

THERE IS NO FRIGATE LIKE A BOOK
EMILY DICKINSON

There is no frigate like a book
    To take us lands away,
Nor any coursers like a page
    Of prancing poetry.
This traverse may the poorest take
    Without oppress of toll;
How frugal is the chariot
    That bears a human soul!

◎

THE SONG OF WANDERING AENGUS
WILLIAM BUTLER YEATS

I went out to the hazel wood,
Because a fire was in my head,
And cut and peeled a hazel wand,
And hooked a berry to a thread;

And when white moths were on the wing,
And moth-like stars were flickering out,
I dropped the berry in a stream
And caught a little silver trout.

When I had laid it on the floor
I went to blow the fire a-flame,
But something rustled on the floor,
And someone called me by my name:
It had become a glimmering girl
With apple blossom in her hair
Who called me by my name and ran
And faded through the brightening air.

Though I am old with wandering
Through hollow lands and hilly lands,
I will find out where she has gone,
And kiss her lips and take her hands;
And walk among long dappled grass,
And pluck till time and times are done,
The silver apples of the moon,
The golden apples of the sun.

○

FROM ROADS GO EVER EVER ON

J. R. R. TOLKIEN

Roads go ever ever on,
Over rock and under tree,
By caves where never sun has shone,
By streams that never find the sea;
Over snow by winter sown,
And through the merry flowers of June,
Over grass and over stone,
And under mountains in the moon.

Roads go ever ever on,
Under cloud and under star.
Yet feet that wandering have gone
Turn at last to home afar.
Eyes that fire and sword have seen,
And horror in the halls of stone
Look at last on meadows green,
And trees and hills they long have known.

The Road goes ever on and on
Down from the door where it began.

Now far ahead the Road has gone,
And I must follow, if I can,
Pursuing it with eager feet,
Until it joins some larger way,
Where many paths and errands meet.

The Road goes ever on and on
Down from the door where it began.
Now far ahead the Road has gone,
And I must follow, if I can,
Pursuing it with weary feet,
Until it joins some larger way,
Where many paths and errands meet.
And whither then? I cannot say.

The Road goes ever on and on
Out from the door where it began.
Now far ahead the Road has gone.
Let others follow, if they can!
Let them a journey new begin.
But I at last with weary feet
Will turn toward the lighted inn,
My evening-rest and sleep to meet.

Still 'round the corner there may wait
A new road or secret gate;
And though I oft have passed them by,
A day will come at last when I
Shall take the hidden paths that run
West of the Moon, East of the Sun.

○

THE ROAD NOT TAKEN
ROBERT FROST

Two roads diverged in a yellow wood,
And sorry I could not travel both
And be one traveler, long I stood
And looked down one as far as I could
To where it bent in the undergrowth;

Then took the other, as just as fair,
And having perhaps the better claim,
Because it was grassy and wanted wear;
Though as for that the passing there
Had worn them really about the same,

And both that morning equally lay
In leaves no step had trodden black.
Oh, I kept the first for another day!
Yet knowing how way leads on to way,
I doubted if I should ever come back.

I shall be telling this with a sigh
Somewhere ages and ages hence:
Two roads diverged in a wood, and I—
I took the one less traveled by,
And that has made all the difference.

HIGH FLIGHT

JOHN GILLESPIE MAGEE, JR.

Oh! I have slipped the surly bonds of Earth
And danced the skies on laughter-silvered wings;
Sunward I've climbed and joined the tumbling mirth
Of sun-split clouds,—and done a hundred things
You have not dreamed of—wheeled and soared and swung
High in the sunlit silence. Hov'ring there,
I've chased the shouting wind along and flung
My eager craft through footless halls of air . . .

Up, up the long, delirious, burning blue
I've topped the wind-swept heights with easy grace
Where never lark, or even eagle flew—
And, while with silent, lifting mind I've trod
The high untrespassed sanctity of space,
Put out my hand, and touched the face of God.

○

SEA-FEVER

JOHN MASEFIELD

I must go down to the seas again, to the lonely sea and the sky,
And all I ask is a tall ship and a star to steer her by,
And the wheel's kick and the wind's song and the white sail's shaking,
And a gray mist on the sea's face, and a gray dawn breaking.

I must go down to the seas again, for the call of the running tide
Is a wild call and a clear call that may not be denied;
And all I ask is a windy day with the white clouds flying,
And the flung spray and the blown spume, and the sea-gulls crying.

I must go down to the seas again, to the vagrant gypsy life,
To the gull's way and the whale's way, where the wind's like a whetted knife;
And all I ask is a merry yarn from a laughing fellow-rover,
And quiet sleep and a sweet dream when the long trick's over.

CARGOES

JOHN MASEFIELD

Quinquireme of Nineveh from distant Ophir,
Rowing home to haven in sunny Palestine,
With a cargo of ivory,
And apes and peacocks,
Sandalwood, cedar wood, and sweet white wine.

Stately Spanish galleon coming from the Isthmus
Dipping through the Tropics by palm-green shores,
With a cargo of diamonds,
Emeralds, amethysts,
Topazes, and cinnamon, and gold moidores.

Dirty British coaster with a salt-caked smoke stack,
Butting through the Channel in the mad March days,
With a cargo of Tyne coal,
Road-rails, pig-lead,
Firewood, iron-ware, and cheap tin trays.

◎

THE DAY MILLICENT FOUND THE WORLD

WILLIAM STAFFORD

Every morning Millicent ventured farther
into the woods. At first she stayed
near light, the edge where bushes grew, where
her way back appeared in glimpses among
dark trunks behind her. Then by farther paths
or openings where giant pines had fallen
she explored ever deeper into
the interior, till one day she stood under a great
dome among columns, the heart of the forest, and knew:
Lost. She had achieved a mysterious world
where any direction would yield only surprise.

And now not only the giant trees were strange
but the ground at her feet had a velvet nearness;
intricate lines on bark wove messages all
around her. Long strokes of golden sunlight
shifted over her feet and hands. She felt
caught up and breathing in a great powerful embrace.
A birdcall wandered forth at leisurely intervals
from an opening on her right: "Come away, Come away."
Never before had she let herself realize
that she was part of the world and that it would follow
wherever she went. She was part of its breath.

Aunt Dolbee called her back that time, a high
voice tapering faintly among the farthest trees,
"Milli-cent! Milli-cent!" And that time she returned,
but slowly, her dress fluttering along pressing
back branches, her feet stirring up the dark smell
of moss, and her face floating forward, a stranger's
face now, with a new depth in it, into the light.

○

SOMETHING THAT HAPPENS RIGHT NOW
WILLIAM STAFFORD

I haven't told this before. By our house on the plains before I was
born my father planted a maple. At night after bedtime when
others were asleep I would go out and stand beside it and know all
the way north and all the way south. Air from the fields wandered
in. Stars waited with me. All of us ached with a silence, needing the
next thing, but quiet. We leaned into midnight and then leaned
back. On the rise to the west the radio tower blinked—so many
messages pouring by.

A great surge came rushing from everywhere and wrapped
all the land and sky. Where were we going? How soon would our
house break loose and become a little speck lost in the vast night?
My father and mother would die. The maple tree would stand right

there. With my hand on that smooth bark we would watch it all.
Then my feet would come loose from Earth and rise by the power
of longing. I wouldn't let the others know about this, but I would
be everywhere, as I am right now, a thin tone like the wind, a sip of
blue light—no source, no end, no horizon.

○

THE LAKE ISLE OF INNISFREE
WILLIAM BUTLER YEATS

I will arise and go now, and go to Innisfree,
And a small cabin build there, of clay and wattles made:
Nine bean-rows will I have there, a hive for the honeybee,
And live alone in the bee-loud glade.
And I shall have some peace there, for peace comes dropping slow,
Dropping from the veils of the morning to where the cricket sings;
There midnight's all a glimmer, and noon a purple glow,
And evening full of the linnet's wings.
I will arise and go now, for always night and day
I hear lake water lapping with low sounds by the shore;
While I stand on the roadway, or on the pavements gray,
I hear it in the deep heart's core.

○

THE HOUSE AND THE ROAD
JOSEPHINE PRESTON PEABODY

The little Road says, Go,
The little House says, Stay:
And O, it's bonny here at home,
But I must go away.

The little Road, like me,
Would seek and turn and know;
And forth I must, to learn the things
The little Road would show!

And go I must, my dears,
And journey while I may,
Though heart be sore for the little House
That had no word but Stay.

Maybe, no other way
Your child could ever know
Why a little House would have you stay,
When a little Road says, Go.

◎

SONG OF THE ROAD
JAMES WHITCOMB RILEY

O I will walk with you, my lad, whichever way you fare,
You'll have me, too, the side o' you, with heart as light as air;
No care for where the road you take's a-leadin' anywhere,—
It can but be a joyful ja'nt whilst you journey there.
The road you take's the path o' love, an' that's the bridth o' two—
An' I will walk with you, my lad—O I will walk with you.

Ho! I will walk with you, my lad,
Be weather black or blue
Or roadsides frost or dew, my lad—
O I will walk with you.

Aye, glad, my lad, I'll walk with you, whatever winds may blow,
Or summer blossoms stay our steps, or blinding drifts of snow;
The way that you set face an' foot 's the way that I will go,
An' brave I'll be, abreast o' ye, the Saints and Angels know!
With loyal hand in loyal hand, an' one heart made o' two,
Through summer's gold, or winter's cold, It's I will walk with you.

Sure, I will walk with you, my lad,
A love ordains me to,—
To Heaven's door, an' through, my lad.
O I will walk with you.

THE BIG ROCK CANDY MOUNTAIN

TRADITIONAL HOBO BALLAD

One evening as the sun went down
And the jungle fire was burning,
Down the track came a hobo hiking,
And he said, "boys I'm not turning.
I'm headed for a land that's far away
Beside the crystal fountains.
So come with me,
We'll go and see
The big rock candy mountains."

In the big rock candy mountains,
There's a land that's fair and bright,
Where the hand-outs grow on bushes
And you sleep out every night;
Where the boxcars all are empty,
And the sun shines every day
On the birds and the bees
And the cigarette trees
The lemonade springs
Where the blue bird sings
In the big rock candy mountains.

In the big rock candy mountains,
All the cops have wooden legs
And the bulldogs all have rubber teeth
And the hens lay soft-boiled eggs.
The farmer's trees are full of fruit
And the barns are full of hay.
O I'm bound to go
Where there ain't no snow
Where the rain don't fall,
And the wind don't blow
In the big rock candy mountains.

In the big rock candy mountains,
You never change your socks
And the little streams of alcohol
Come a-trickling down the rocks.
The brakemen have to tip their hats,
And the railroad bulls are blind,
There's a lake of stew,
And of whiskey, too
You can paddle all around 'em
In a big canoe
In the big rock candy mountains.

In the big rock candy mountains,
The jails are made of tin,
And you can walk right out again
As soon as you are in.
There ain't no short-handled shovels,
No axes, saws or picks.
I'm a-goin' to stay
Where you sleep all day
Where they hung the jerk
That invented work
In the big rock candy mountains.

I'll see you all
this comin' fall
In the big rock candy mountains.

XI
True Love

Love goes toward love
as school boys from their books.
But love from love, toward school
with heavy looks.

—WILLIAM SHAKESPEARE, FROM ROMEO AND JULIET

I LOVE THEE—I LOVE THEE!

NEVER SEEK TO TELL THY LOVE
WILLIAM BLAKE

Never seek to tell thy love,
Love that never told can be;
For the gentle wind doth move
Silently, invisibly.

⊙

FROM I LOVE THEE
THOMAS HOOD

I love thee—I love thee!
'Tis all that I can say;
It is my vision in the night,
My dreaming in the day;
The very echo of my heart,
The blessing when I pray:
I love thee—I love thee!
Is all that I can say.

⊙

ANSWER TO A CHILD'S QUESTION
SAMUEL TAYLOR COLERIDGE

Do you ask what the birds say? The Sparrow, the Dove,
The Linnet and Thrush say, "I love and I love!"
In the winter they're silent—the wind is so strong;
What it says, I don't know, but it sings a loud song.
But green leaves, and blossoms, and sunny warm weather,
And singing, and loving—all come back together.
But the Lark is so brimful of gladness and love,
The green fields below him, the blue sky above,
That he sings, and he sings; and for ever sings he—
"I love my Love, and my Love loves me!"

DRINK TO ME ONLY WITH THINE EYES

FROM "TO CELIA"
BEN JONSON

Drink to me only with thine eyes,
    And I will pledge with mine.
Or leave a kiss but in the cup
    And I'll not look for wine.
The thirst that from the soul doth rise
    Doth ask a drink divine;
But might I of Jove's nectar sup
    I would not change for thine.

○

RONDEAU

JAMES HENRY LEIGH HUNT

Jenny kissed me when we met,
Jumping from the chair she sat in;
Time, you thief, who love to get
Sweets into your list, put that in:
Say I'm weary, say I'm sad,
Say that health and wealth have missed me,
Say I'm growing old, but add,
Jenny kissed me.

HONEYSUCKLE

WILLIAM STAFFORD

Not yet old enough, still only a kid,
you meet Hazel. She is not old enough either—
it is the world before: it is early. The two of you
walk through slow, heavy, thick air.

Now you are coming to the corner where
                                 hummingbirds have
their nest. You breathe. It is the honeysuckle
tangled along the church wall. Each of you
takes a blossom to taste as you say goodby.

That flavor last a long time. Forever.

◎

THE GOOD-MORROW

JOHN DONNE

I wonder, by my troth, what thou and I
Did, till we loved? were we not weaned till then?
But sucked on country pleasures, childishly?
Or snorted we in the Seven Sleepers' den?
'Twas so; but this, all pleasures fancies be.
If ever any beauty I did see,
Which I desired, and got, 'twas but a dream of thee.

And now good-morrow to our waking souls,
Which watch not one another out of fear;
For love, all love of other sights controls,
And makes one little room an everywhere.
Let sea-discoverers to new worlds have gone,
Let maps to others, worlds on worlds have shown,
Let us possess one world, each hath one, and is one.

My face in thine eye, thine in mine appears,
And true plain hearts do in the faces rest;
Where can we find two better hemispheres,
Without sharp north, without declining west?
Whatever dies was not mixed equally;
If our two loves be one, or, thou and I
Love so alike that none do slacken, none can die.

◯

IN MY CRAFT OR SULLEN ART
DYLAN THOMAS

In my craft or sullen art
Exercised in the still night
When only the moon rages
And the lovers lie abed
With all their griefs in their arms
I labor by singing light
Not for ambition or bread
Or the strut and trade of charms
On the ivory stages
But for the common wages
Of their most secret heart.

Not for the proud man apart
From the raging moon I write
On these spindrift pages
Nor for the towering dead
With their nightingales and psalms
But for the lovers, their arms
Round the griefs of the ages,
Who pay no praise or wages
Nor heed my craft or art.

A RED, RED ROSE

ROBERT BURNS

Oh my luve is like a red, red rose,
That's newly sprung in June:
Oh my luve is like the melodie,
That's sweetly play'd in tune.

As fair art thou, my bonie lass,
So deep in luve am I;
And I will luve thee still, my dear,
Till a' the seas gang dry.

Till a' the seas gang dry, my dear,
And the rocks melt wi' the sun;
And I will luve thee still, my dear,
While the sands o' life shall run.

And fare thee weel, my only luve!
And fare thee weel a while!
And I will come again, my luve,
Tho' it were ten thousand mile!

SONNET 12
WILLIAM SHAKESPEARE

Shall I compare thee to a summer's day?
Thou art more lovely and more temperate:
Rough winds do shake the darling buds of May,
And summer's lease hath all too short a date:
Sometimes too hot the eye of heaven shines,
And often is his gold complexion dimmed;
And every fair from fair sometimes declines,
By chance or nature's changing course untrimmed;
But thy eternal summer shall not fade,
Nor lose possession of that fair thou ow'st;
Nor shall death brag thou wander'st in his shade
When in eternal lines to time thou grow'st:
So long as men can breathe, or eyes can see,
So long lives this, and this gives life to thee.

◎

HOW DO I LOVE THEE?
ELIZABETH BARRETT BROWNING

How do I love thee? Let me count the ways.
I love thee to the depth and breadth and height
My soul can reach, when feeling out of sight
For the ends of Being and ideal Grace.
I love thee to the level of every day's
Most quiet need, by sun and candlelight.
I love thee freely, as men strive for Right;
I love thee purely, as they turn from Praise.
I love with a passion put to use
In my old griefs, and with my childhood's faith.
I love thee with a love I seemed to lose
With my lost saints,—I love thee with the breath,
Smiles, tears, of all my life!—and, if God choose,
I shall but love thee better after death.

ANNABEL LEE

EDGAR ALLAN POE

It was many and many a year ago,
In a kingdom by the sea,
That a maiden there lived whom you may know
By the name of Annabel Lee;
And this maiden she lived with no other thought
Than to love and be loved by me.

I was a child and she was a child,
In this kingdom by the sea;
But we loved with a love that was more than love—
I and my Annabel Lee;
With a love that the winged seraphs of heaven
Coveted her and me.

And this was the reason that, long ago,
In this kingdom by the sea,
A wind blew out of a cloud, chilling
My beautiful Annabel Lee;
So that her highborn kinsman came
And bore her away from me,
To shut her up in a sepulchre
In this kingdom by the sea.

The angels, not half so happy in heaven,
Went envying her and me—
Yes!—that was the reason (as all men know,
In this kingdom by the sea)
That the wind came out of the cloud by night,
Chilling and killing my Annabel Lee.

But our love it was stronger by far than the love
Of those who were older than we—
Of many far wiser than we—
And neither the angels in heaven above,
Nor the demons down under the sea,
Can ever dissever my soul from the soul
Of the beautiful Annabel Lee.

For the moon never beams without bringing me dreams
Of the beautiful Annabel Lee;
And the stars never rise but I feel the bright eyes
Of the beautiful Annabel Lee;
And so, all the night-tide, I lie down by the side
Of my darling—my darling—my life and my bride,
In the sepulchre there by the sea,
In her tomb by the sounding sea.

○

THE RAGGLE, TAGGLE GYPSIES
EIGHTEENTH-CENTURY TRADITONAL FOLK BALLAD

There were three gypsies a-come to my door,
    And downstairs ran this lady, O.
One sang high and another sang low,
    And the other sang "Bonnie, Bonnie Biskay, O."

Then she pulled off her silken gown,
    And put on hose of leather, O.
With the ragged, ragged rags about her door
    She's off with the Raggle, Taggle Gypsies, O.

'Twas late last night when my lord came home,
    Inquiring for his lady, O.
The servants said on every hand,
    "She's gone with the Raggle, Taggle Gypsies, O."

"Oh, saddle for me my milk-white steed,
    Oh, saddle for me my pony, O,
That I may ride and seek my bride
    Who's gone with the Raggle, Taggle Gypsies, O."

Oh, he rode high and he rode low,
    He rode through woods and copses, O,
Until he came to an open field,
    And there he espied his lady, O.

"What makes you leave your house and lands?
    What makes you leave your money, O?
What makes you leave your new-wedded lord
    To go with the Raggle, Taggle Gypsies, O?"

"What care I for my house and lands?
    What care I for my money, O?
What care I for my new-wedded lord?
    I'm off with the Raggle, Taggle Gypsies, O."

"Last night you slept on a goose-feather bed,
    With the sheet turned down so bravely, O.
Tonight you will sleep in the cold, open field,
    Along with the Raggle, Taggle Gypsies, O."

"What care I for your goose-feather bed,
    With the sheet turned down so bravely, O?
For tonight I shall sleep in a cold, open field,
    Along with the Raggle, Taggle Gypsies, O."

LOCHINVAR

SIR WALTER SCOTT

O, young Lochinvar is come out of the west,
Through all the wide Border his steed was the best,
And save his good broadsword he weapons had none;
He rode all unarmed, and he rode all alone.
So faithful in love, and so dauntless in war,
There never was knight like the young Lochinvar.

He stayed not for brake, and he stopped not for stone,
He swam the Eske river where ford there was none;
But, ere he alighted at Netherby gate,
The bride had consented, the gallant came late:
For a laggard in love, and a dastard in war,
Was to wed the fair Ellen of brave Lochinvar.

So boldly he entered the Netherby hall,
Among bride's-men and kinsmen, and brothers and all;
Then spoke the bride's father, his hand on his sword
(For the poor craven bridegroom said never a word),
"O come ye in peace here, or come ye in war,
Or to dance at our bridal, young Lord Lochinvar?"

"I long wooed your daughter, my suit you denied;—
Love swells like the Solway, but ebbs like its tide—
And now I am come, with this lost love of mine,
To lead but one measure, drink one cup of wine.
There are maidens in Scotland more lovely by far,
That would gladly be bride to the young Lochinvar."

The bride kissed the goblet; the knight took it up,
He quaffed off the wine, and he threw down the cup,
She looked down to blush; and she looked up to sigh,
With a smile on her lips and a tear in her eye.
He took her soft hand, ere her mother could bar,—
"Now tread we a measure!" said young Lochinvar.

So stately his form, and so lovely her face,
That never a hall such a galliard did grace;
While her mother did fret, and her father did fume,
And the bridegroom stood dangling his bonnet and plume;
And the bride-maidens whispered, " 'Twere better by far
To have matched our fair cousin with young Lochinvar."

One touch to her hand, and one word in her ear,
When they reached the hall door, and the charger stood near:
So light to the croupe the fair lady he swung,
So light to the saddle before her he sprung!
"She is won! we are gone, over bank, bush, and scaur;
They'll have fleet steeds that follow," quoth young Lochinvar.

There was mounting 'mong Graemes of the Netherby clan;
Forsters, Fenwicks, and Musgraves, they rode and they ran;
There was racing, and chasing, on Cannobie Lee,
But the lost bride of Netherby ne'er did they see.
So daring in love, and so dauntless in war,
Have ye e'er heard of gallant like young Lochinvar?

☉

THE OWL AND THE PUSSYCAT
EDWARD LEAR

The Owl and the Pussycat went to sea
    In a beautiful pea-green boat:
They took some honey, and plenty of money
    Wrapped up in a five-pound note.
The Owl looked up to the stars above,
    And sang to a small guitar,
"O lovely Pussy, O Pussy, my love,
    What a beautiful Pussy you are,
            You are,
            You are!
    What a beautiful Pussy you are!"

Pussy said to the Owl, "You elegant fowl,
   How charmingly sweet you sing!
Oh! Let us be married; too long we have tarried:
   But what shall we do for a ring?"
They sailed away, for a year and a day,
   To the land where the bong tree grows;
And there in a wood a Piggy-wig stood,
   With a ring at the end of his nose,
          His nose,
          His nose,
   With a ring at the end of his nose.

"Dear Pig, are you willing to sell for one shilling
   Your ring?" Said the Piggy, "I will."
So they took it away, and were married next day
   By the Turkey who lives on the hill.
They dined on mince and slices of quince,
   Which they ate with a runcible spoon;
And hand in hand, on the edge of the sand,
   They danced by the light of the moon,
          The moon,
          The moon,
   They danced by the light of the moon.

XII
Creator & Creation

I do not know how I may appear
to the world; but to myself I seem
To have been only like a boy,
playing on the seashore...

—*SIR ISAAC NEWTON*

PETER THE SEA-BOY DANCED AND PRANCED
AND SANG HIS RIDDLE-CUM-REE.

I DO NOT KNOW HOW I MAY APPEAR TO THE WORLD

SIR ISAAC NEWTON

I do not know how I may appear to the world; but to myself I seem to have been only like a boy, playing on the seashore, and diverting myself, in now and then finding another pebble or prettier shell than ordinary, while the great ocean of truth lay all undiscovered before me.

⊙

FROM VOLPOSA

OLD NORSE HYMN OF THE DOOM

Before the years, when Naught was; was neither sand nor sea nor cold billows; earth was seen not, nor high heaven; there was the gap gapping, and grass nowhere.

⊙

BLESSED IS HE WHO MADE THE CONSTELLATIONS

FROM THE KORAN, 25:61

Blessed is He who made the constellations in the heavens and made therein a lamp and a shining moon.

⊙

AND THE LORD GOD FORMED MAN

FROM THE KING JAMES VERSION OF THE BIBLE, GENESIS 3:7

And the Lord God formed man
Of the dust of the ground,
And breathed into his nostrils the breath of life;
And man became a living soul.

THE COMING OF THE TREES

ARTHUR GUITERMAN

"Let trees be made, for earth is bare,"
Spake the voice of the Lord in thunder:
The roots ran deep, the trees were there,
And earth was full of wonder.

For the white birch leaned, the oak held straight,
The pines marched down the mountain,
The orchards bowed with their blossomed weight
And the elm rose up like a fountain.

The palm stood proud as Aaron's rod,
The willow billowed slowly;
So came the trees at the call of God,
And all the trees are holy.

○

THE LAMB

WILLIAM BLAKE

Little Lamb, who made thee?
Dost thou know who made thee?
Gave thee life and bid thee feed,
By the stream & o'er the mead;
Gave thee clothing of delight,
Softest clothing wooly bright;
Gave thee such a tender voice,
Making all the vales rejoice!
Little Lamb who made thee?
Dost thou know who made thee?

Little Lamb I'll tell thee,
Little Lamb I'll tell thee!
He is called by thy name,
For he calls himself a Lamb:
He is meek and he is mild,
He became a little child:
I a child & thou a lamb,
We are called by his name.
Little Lamb God bless thee.
Little Lamb God bless thee.

○

THE TYGER

WILLIAM BLAKE

Tyger! Tyger! burning bright
In the forests of the night,
What immortal hand or eye
Could frame thy fearful symmetry?

In what distant deeps or skies
Burnt the fire of thine eyes?
On what wings dare he aspire?
What the hand dare seize the fire?

And what shoulder, & what art,
Could twist the sinews of thy heart?
And when thy heart began to beat,
What dread hand? & what dread feet?

What the hammer? what the chain?
In what furnace was thy brain?
What the anvil? what dread grasp
Dare its deadly terrors clasp?

When the stars threw down their spears,
And water'd heaven with their tears,
Did he smile his work to see?
Did he who made the Lamb make thee?

Tyger! Tyger! burning bright
In the forests of the night,
What immortal hand or eye
Dare frame thy fearful symmetry?

○

THE WOLF ALSO SHALL DWELL WITH THE LAMB
FROM THE KING JAMES VERSION OF THE BIBLE, ISAIAH 11:6

The wolf also shall dwell with the lamb,
and the leopard shall lie down with the kid;
and the calf and the young lion
and the fatling together;
and a little child shall lead them.

○

UNLESS YE BECOME AS A LITTLE CHILD
FROM THE KING JAMES VERSION OF THE BIBLE, MATTHEW 18:3

Unless ye become as a little child
ye shall not enter the kingdom of heaven.

THE STAR

JANE TAYLOR

Twinkle, twinkle, little star,
How I wonder what you are!
Up above the world so high,
Like a diamond in the sky.

When the blazing sun is gone,
When he nothing shines upon,
Then you show your little light,
Twinkle, twinkle, all the night.

Then the traveler in the dark,
Thanks you for your tiny spark,
He could not see which way to go,
If you did not twinkle so.

In the dark blue sky you keep,
And often through my curtains peep,
For you never shut your eye,
Till the sun is in the sky.

As your bright and tiny spark,
Lights the traveler in the dark—
Though I know not what you are,
Twinkle, twinkle, little star.

THE EARTH ABIDETH FOREVER

FROM THE KING JAMES VERSION OF THE BIBLE, ECCLESIASTES 1:4

The earth abideth forever.
The sun also ariseth, and the sun goeth down,
And hasteth to his place where he arose.

The wind goeth toward the south,
And turneth about unto the north;
It whirleth about continually,
And the wind returneth again according to his circuits.

All the rivers run into the sea;
Yet the sea is not full;
Unto the place whence the rivers come,
Thither they return again.

○

THE NEGRO SPEAKS OF RIVERS

LANGSTON HUGHES

I've known rivers:
I've known rivers ancient as the world and older than
        the flow of human blood in human veins.

My soul has grown deep like the rivers.

I bathed in the Euphrates when dawns were young.
I built my hut near the Congo and it lulled me to sleep.
I looked upon the Nile and raised the pyramids above it.
I heard the singing of the Mississippi when Abe Lincoln went down
        to New Orleans, and I've seen its muddy bosom turn all golden
        in the sunset.

I've known rivers:
Ancient, dusky rivers.

My soul has grown deep like the rivers.

DAYBREAK

GALWAY KINNELL

On the tidal mud, just before sunset,
dozens of starfishes
were creeping. It was as though the mud were a sky
and enormous, imperfect stars
moved across it as slowly
as the actual stars cross heaven.
All at once they stopped,
and as if they had simply
increased their receptivity
to gravity they sank down
into the mud; they faded down
into it and lay still; and by the time
pink of sunset broke across them
they were as invisible
as the true stars at daybreak.

○

SONG FOR THE SUN THAT DISAPPEARED BEHIND THE RAIN CLOUDS

The fire darkens, the wood turns black,
The flame extinguishes, misfortune upon us.
God sets out in search of the sun.
The rainbow sparkles in his hand,
The bow of the divine hunter.
He has heard the lamentations of his children.
He walks along the milky way, he collects the stars.
With quick arms he piles them into a basket
Piles them up with quick arms
Like a woman who collects lizards
And piles them into her pot, piles them
Until the pot overflows with lizards
Until the basket overflows with light.

I'M AN INDIAN

JOHN LAME DEER

I'm an Indian.
I think about ordinary, common things like this pot.
The bubbling water comes from the rain cloud.
It represents the sky.
The fire comes from the sun
which warms us all—men, animals, trees.
The meat stands for the four-legged creatures,
our animal brothers,
who gave of themselves so that we should live.
The steam is living breath.
It was water, now it goes up to the sky,
becomes a cloud again.
These things are sacred.
Looking at that pot full of good soup,
I am thinking how, in this simple manner,
the great Spirit takes care of me.

○

MASTER OF THE UNIVERSE

RABBI NACHMAN OF BRESLOV

Master of the Universe
Grant me the ability to be alone;
May it be my custom to go outdoors each day
Among the trees and grasses,
Among all growing things
And there may I be alone,
And enter into prayer
To talk with the one
That I belong to.

THE LORD IS MY SHEPHERD

FROM THE BIBLE, PSALM 23

The Lord is my shepherd;
I shall not want.
He maketh me to lie down in green pastures;
He leadeth me beside the still waters.
He restoreth my soul.

He leadeth me in the paths of righteousness
For his name's sake.
Yea, though I walk through the valley of the shadow of death,
I will fear no evil:
For thou art with me;
Thy rod and thy staff
They comfort me.

Thou preparest a table before me
In the presence of mine enemies;
Thou anointest my head with oil;
My cup runneth over.

Surely goodness and mercy shall follow me
All the days of my life:
And I will dwell in the house of the Lord
For ever.

TEACH YOUR CHILDREN
ATTRIBUTED TO CHIEF SEATTLE

Teach your children
what we have taught our children—
that the earth is our mother.
Whatever befalls the earth
befalls the sons and daughters of the earth.
If men spit upon the ground,
they spit upon themselves.

This we know.
The earth does not belong to us;
we belong to the earth.
This we know.
All things are connected
like the blood which unites one family.
All things are connected.

Whatever befalls the earth
befalls the sons and daughters of the earth.
We did not weave the web of life;
We are merely a strand in it.
Whatever we do to the web,
we do to ourselves....

THE HUNTING PRAYER
LARRY LITTLEBIRD

Look at you, magnificent creature lying there,
How is it that we, your poor human brothers,
Could be worthy to borrow
Your life? You honor us, you allow us
To witness the power and magnificence
Of the Creator. God has blessed
Your life and we see that.
Thank God for the continued
Sustenance that is provided
For all our relations:
The sun, the clouds, the rain,
The snow, the water, the air,
The earth and the mystery of fire.
Now we are going to carry
You home; you come with us easily.
Our people will be
Happy to see you.
They will make you welcome.
You will live again
In all our lives, my brother.

○

WHEN YOU WALK ACROSS THE FIELDS
HASIDIC SAYING

When you walk across the fields with your mind pure and holy,
then from all the stones, and all growing things, and all animals,
the sparks of their souls come out and cling to you, and then they
are purified and become a holy fire in you.

PIED BEAUTY

GERARD MANLEY HOPKINS

Glory be to God for dappled things—
    For skies of couple-color as a brinded cow;
      For rose-moles all in stipple upon trout that swim;
Fresh-firecoal chestnut-falls; finches' wings;
    Landscaped plotted and pieced—fold, fallow, and plow;
      And all trades, their gear and tackle and trim.

All things counter, original, spare, strange;
    Whatever is fickle, freckled (who knows how?)
      With swift, slow; sweet, sour; adazzle, dim;
He fathers-forth whose beauty is past change:
    Praise Him.

XIII
Seasons of Life

... as I stared, he slowly changed,
for he was growing backward into youth,
and when he had become a boy,
I knew that he was myself with all the
years that would be mine at last.
—FROM BLACK ELK SPEAKS BY JOHN NEIHARDT

A THOUSANDS DOORS AGO / WHEN I WAS A LONELY KID /
IN A BIG HOUSE WITH FOUR / GARAGES...

IT WAS WHEN I WAS FIVE YEARS OLD

FROM BLACK ELK SPEAKS
JOHN G. NEIHARDT

It was when I was five years old that my Grandfather made me a
bow and some arrows. The grass was young and I was horseback. A
thunder storm was coming from where the sun goes down, and just
as I was riding into the woods along a creek, there was a kingbird
sitting on a limb. This was not a dream, it happened. And I was
going to shoot at the kingbird with the bow my Grandfather made,
when the bird spoke and said: "The clouds all over are one-sided."
Perhaps it meant that all the clouds were looking at me. And then it
said: "Listen! A voice is calling you!" Then I looked up at the clouds,
and two men were coming there, headfirst like arrows slanting
down; and as they came, they sang a sacred song and the thunder
was like drumming. I will sing it for you. The song and drumming
were like this:

> "Behold, a sacred voice is calling you;
>   All over the sky a sacred voice is calling."

I sat there gazing at them, and they were coming from the place
where the giant lives (north). But when they were very close to me,
they wheeled about toward where the sun goes down, and suddenly
they were geese. Then they were gone, and the rain came with a big
wind and a roaring.

I did not tell this vision to any one. I liked to think about it, but
I was afraid to tell it.

NOW SUDDENLY THERE WAS NOTHING BUT
A WORLD OF CLOUD

FROM BLACK ELK SPEAKS
JOHN G. NEIHARDT

Now suddenly there was nothing but a world of cloud, and we three
were there alone in the middle of a great white plain with snowy
hills and mountains staring at us; and it was very still; but there
were whispers.

Then the two men spoke together and they said: "Behold him,
the being with four legs!"

I looked and saw a bay horse standing there, and he began to
speak: "Behold me!" he said. "My life-history you shall see." Then
he wheeled about to where the sun goes down, and said: "Behold
them! Their history you shall know."

I looked, and there were twelve black horses yonder all abreast
with necklaces of bison hoofs, and they were beautiful, but I was
frightened, because their manes were lightning and there was
thunder in their nostrils....

And when I had seen all these the bay horse said: "Your
grandfathers are having a council. These shall take you; so have
courage."

○

NOW I KNEW THE SIXTH GRANDFATHER WAS
ABOUT TO SPEAK

FROM BLACK ELK SPEAKS
JOHN G. NEIHARDT

Now I knew the sixth grandfather was about to speak, he who was
the spirit of the earth, and I saw that he was very old, but more
as men are old. His hair was long and white, his face was all in
wrinkles and his eyes were deep and dim. I stared at him, for it
seemed I knew him somehow, and as I stared he slowly changed,
for he was growing backwards into youth, and when he had become
a boy, I knew he was myself with all the years that would be mine at
last. When he was old again, he said: "My boy, have courage, for my

power shall be yours, and you shall need it, for your nation on the earth will have great troubles. Come."

He rose and tottered out through the rainbow door, and as I followed I was riding on the bay horse who had talked to me at first and led me to that place.

○

THE RAINBOW
WILLIAM WORDSWORTH

My heart leaps up when I behold
A rainbow in the sky.
So it was when my life began;
So it is now I am a man;
So be it when I shall grow old,
        Or let me die!
The Child is father of the Man,
And I could wish my days to be
Bound each to each by natural piety.

○

ALL THE WORLD'S A STAGE
FROM AS YOU LIKE IT, ACT II, SCENE VII
WILLIAM SHAKESPEARE

                All the world's a stage,
And all the men and women merely players:
They have their exits and their entrances;
And one man in his time plays many parts,
His acts being seven ages. At first the infant,
Mewling and puking in the nurse's arms.
Then the whining school-boy, with his satchel
And shining morning face, creeping like snail
Unwillingly to school. And then the lover,
Sighing like furnace, with a woeful ballad
Made to his mistress' eyebrow. Then a soldier,

Full of strange oaths, and bearded like the pard,
Jealous in honor, sudden and quick in quarrel,
Seeking the bubble reputation
Even in the cannon's mouth. And then the justice,
in fair round belly with good capon lined,
With eyes severe and beard of formal cut,
Full of wise saws and modern instances;
And so he plays his part. The sixth age shifts
Into the lean and slipper'd pantaloon,
With spectacles on nose and pouch on side,
His youthful hose, well saved, a world too wide
For his shrunk shank; and his big manly voice,
Turning again toward childish treble, pipes
And whistles in his sound. Last scene of all,
That ends this strange eventful history,
Is second childishness and mere oblivion,
Sans teeth, sans eyes, sans taste, sans everything.

○

YOU ARE OLD, FATHER WILLIAM
FROM ALICE'S ADVENTURES IN WONDERLAND
LEWIS CARROLL

"You are old, father William," the young man said,
"And your hair has become very white;
And yet you incessantly stand on your head—
Do you think, at your age, it is right?

"In my youth," father William replied to his son,
"I feared it might injure the brain;
But, now that I'm perfectly sure I have none,
Why, I do it again and again."

"You are old," said the youth, "as I mentioned before,
And you have grown most uncommonly fat;
Yet you turned a back-somersault in at the door—
Pray what is the reason for that?"

"In my youth," said the sage, as he shook his gray locks,
"I kept all my limbs very supple
By the use of this ointment—one shilling a box—
Allow me to sell you a couple?"

"You are old," said the youth, "and your jaws are too weak
For anything tougher than suet;
Yet you finished the goose, with the bones and the beak—
Pray, how did you manage to do it?"

"In my youth," said his father, "I took to the law,
And argued each case with my wife;
And the muscular strength, which it gave to my jaw,
Has lasted the rest of my life."

"You are old," said the youth, "one would hardly suppose
That your eye was as steady as ever;
Yet you balanced an eel on the end of your nose—
What made you so awfully clever?"

"I have answered three questions, and that is enough,"
Said his father. "Don't give yourself airs!
Do you think I can listen all day to such stuff?
Be off, or I'll kick you downstairs."

ELDORADO

EDGAR ALLAN POE

Gaily bedight,
A gallant knight,
In sunshine and in shadow,
Had journeyed long,
Singing a song,
In search of Eldorado.

But he grew old—
This knight so bold—
And o'er his heart a shadow
Fell as he found
No spot of ground
That looked like Eldorado.

And, as his strength
Failed him at length,
He met a pilgrim shadow—
"Shadow," said he,
"Where can it be—
This land of Eldorado?"

"Over the Mountains
Of the Moon,
Down the Valley of the Shadow,
Ride, boldly ride,"
The Shade replied—
"If you seek for Eldorado!"

ENCOUNTER
CZESLAW MILOSZ

We were riding through frozen fields in a wagon at dawn.
A red wing rose in the darkness.

And suddenly a hare ran across the road.
One of us pointed to it with his hand.

That was long age. Today neither of them is alive,
Not the hare, nor the man who made the gesture.

O my love, where are they, where are they going
The flash of a hand, streak of movement, rustle of pebbles.
I ask not out of sorrow, but in wonder.

○

OUR BIRTH IS BUT A SLEEP AND A FORGETTING
FROM ODE: INTIMATIONS OF IMMORTALITY
FROM RECOLLECTIONS OF EARLY CHILDHOOD
WILLIAM WORDSWORTH

Our birth is but a sleep and a forgetting;
The soul that rises with us, our life's star,
          Hath had elsewhere its setting
          And cometh from afar;
     Not in entire forgetfulness,
     And not in utter nakedness,
But trailing clouds of glory do we come
     From God who is our home;
Heaven lies about us in our infancy!
Shades of the prison-house begin to close
     Upon the growing boy.

Fern Hill
DYLAN THOMAS

Now as I was young and easy under the apple boughs
About the lilting house and happy as the grass was green,
   The night above the dingle starry,
      Time let me hail and climb
   Golden in the heydays of his eyes,
And honored among wagons I was prince of the apple towns
And once below a time I lordly had the trees and leaves
      Trail with daisies and barley
   Down the rivers of the windfall light.

And as I was green and carefree, famous among the barns
About the happy yard and singing as the farm was home,
   In the sun that is young once only,
      Time let me play and be
   Golden in the mercy of his means,
And green and golden I was huntsman and herdsman, the calves
Sang to my horn, the foxes on the hills barked clear and cold,
      And the Sabbath rang slowly
   In the pebbles of the holy streams.

All the sun long it was running, it was lovely, the hay
Fields high as the house, the tunes from the chimneys, it was air
   And playing, lovely and watery
      And fire green as grass.
   And nightly under the simple stars
As I rode to sleep the owls were bearing the farm away,
All the moon long I heard, blessed among stables, the nightjars
   Flying with the ricks, and the horses
      Flashing into the dark.

And then to awake, and the farm, like a wanderer white
With the dew, come back, the cock on his shoulder: it was all
   Shining, it was Adam and maiden,
      The sky gathered again
   And the sun grew round that very day.

So it must have been after the birth of the simple light
In the first, spinning place, the spellbound horses walking warm
   Out of the whinnying green stable
      On to the fields of praise.

And honored among foxes and pheasants by the gay house
Under the new made clouds and happy as the heart was long,
   In the sun born over and over,
      I ran my heedless ways,
   My wishes raced through the house high hay
And nothing I cared, at my sky blue trades, that time allows
In all his tuneful turning so few and such morning songs
   Before the children green and golden
      Follow him out of grace.

Nothing I cared, in the lamb white days, that time would take me
Up to the swallow thronged loft by the shadow of my hand,
   In the moon that is always rising,
      Nor that riding to sleep
   I should hear him fly with the high fields
And wake to the farm forever fled from the childless land.
Oh as I was young and easy in the mercy of his means,
      Time held me green and dying
   Though I sang in my chains like the sea.

◎

YOUNG

ANNE SEXTON

A thousand doors ago
when I was a lonely kid
in a big house with four
garages and it was summer
as long as I could remember,
I lay on the lawn at night,

clover wrinkling under me,
the wise stars bedding over me,
my mother's window a funnel
of yellow heat running out,
my father's window, half shut,
an eye where sleepers pass,
and the boards of the house
were smooth and white as wax
and probably a million leaves
sailed on their strange stalks
as the crickets ticked together
and I, in my brand new body,
which was not a woman's yet,
told the stars my questions
and thought God could really see
the heat and the painted light,
elbow, knees, dreams, goodnight.

○

IT WAS THE WIND THAT GAVE THEM LIFE
NAVAJO CHANT

It was the wind that gave them life.
It is the wind that comes out of our mouths now
that gives us life.
When this ceases to blow we die.
In the skin at the tips of our fingers
we see the trail of the wind,
it shows us the wind blew
when our ancestors were created.

DO NOT GO GENTLE INTO THAT GOOD NIGHT
DYLAN THOMAS

Do not go gentle into that good night,
Old age should burn and rave at close of day;
Rage, rage against the dying of the light.

Though wise men at their end know dark is right,
Because their words had forked no lightning they
Do not go gentle into that good night.

Good men, the last wave by, crying how bright
Their frail deeds might have danced in a green bay,
Rage, rage against the dying of the light.

Wild men who caught and sang the sun in flight,
And learn, too late, they grieved it on its way,
Do not go gentle into that good night.

Grave men, near death, who see with blinding sight
Blind eyes could blaze like meteors and be gay,
Rage, rage against the dying of the light.

And you, my father, there on that sad height,
Curse, bless, me now with your fierce tears, I pray.
Do not go gentle into that good night.
Rage, rage against the dying of the light.

◎

DEATH BE NOT PROUD
JOHN DONNE

Death be not proud, though some have called thee
Mighty and dreadfull, for, thou art not soe,
For, those, whom thou think'st, thou dost overthrow,
Die not, poore death, nor yet canst thou kill mee.
From rest and sleepe, which but thy pictures bee,
Much pleasure, then from thee, much more must flow,
And soonest our best men with thee doe goe,

Rest of their bones, and soules deliverie.
Thou art slave to Fate, Chance, kings, and desperate men,
And dost with poison, warre, and sicknesse dwell,
And poppie, or charmes can make us sleepe as well,
And better then thy stroake; why swell'st thou then?
One short sleepe past, wee wake eternally,
And death shall be no more; death, thou shalt die.

○

FULL FATHOM FIVE THY FATHER LIES
FROM THE TEMPEST, *ACT I, SCENE II*
WILLIAM SHAKESPEARE

Full fathom five thy father lies;
Of his bones are coral made;
Those are pearls that were his eyes:
Nothing of him that doth fade
But doth suffer a sea-change
Into something rich and strange.
Sea-nymphs hourly ring his knell:
Ding-dong.
Hark! now I hear them,—*ding-dong, bell.*

○

REQUIEM
ROBERT LOUIS STEVENSON

Under the wide and starry sky
Dig the grave and let me lie.
Glad did I live and gladly die,
And I laid me down with a will.

This be the verse you grave for me;
"Here he lies where he longed to be,
Home is the sailor, home from sea,
And the hunter home from the hill."

XIV
Heroes

When I hear the old men
Telling of heroes,
Telling of great deeds
Of ancient days,
When I hear them telling,
Then I think within me
I too am one of these.

—FROM A SONG OF GREATNESS,
A CHIPPEWA INDIAN SONG

I TOO WHEN MY TIME COMES, / SHALL DO MIGHTILY.

A Story That Could Be True

WILLIAM STAFFORD

If you were exchanged in the cradle and
your real mother died
without ever telling the story
then no one knows your name,
and somewhere in the world
your father is lost and needs you
but you are far away.

He can never find
how true you are, how ready.
When the great wind comes
and the robberies of the rain
you stand on the corner shivering.
The people who go by—
you wonder at their calm.

They miss the whisper that runs
any day in your mind,
"Who are you really, wanderer?"—
and the answer you have to give
no matter how dark and cold
the world around you is:
"Maybe I'm a king."

HIAWATHA'S CHILDHOOD
FROM THE SONG OF HIAWATHA
HENRY WADSWORTH LONGFELLOW

By the shores of Gitchee Gumee,
By the shining Big-Sea-Water,
Stood the wigwam of Nokomis
Daughter of the Moon, Nokomis.
Dark behind it rose the forest,
Rose the black and gloomy pine trees,
Rose the firs with cones upon them;
Bright before it beat the water,
Beat the clear and sunny water,
Beat the shining Big-Sea-Water.

There the wrinkled old Nokomis
Nursed the little Hiawatha,
Rocked him in his linden cradle,
Bedded soft in moss and rushes,
Safely bound with reindeer sinews;
Stilled his fretful wail by saying,
"Hush! the Naked Bear will hear thee!"
Lulled him into slumber, singing,
"Ewa-yea! my little owlet!
Who is this that lights the wigwam?
With his great eyes lights the wigwam?
Ewa-yea! my little owlet!"

Many things Nokomis taught him
Of the stars that shine in heaven;
Showed him Ishkoodah, the comet,
Ishkoodah, with fiery tresses;
Showed the Death-Dance of the spirits,
Warriors with their plumes and war-clubs,
Flaring far away to Northward
In the frosty nights of Winter;
Showed the broad white road in heaven,

Pathway of the ghosts, the shadows,
Running straight across the heavens,
Crowded with the ghosts, the shadows.

At the door on Summer evenings
Sat the little Hiawatha;
Heard the whispering of the pine trees,
Heard the lapping of the waters.
Sounds of music, words of wonder;
"Minne-wawa!" said the pine trees,
"Mudway-aushka!" said the water.

Saw the firefly, Wah-wah-taysee,
Flitting through the dusk of evening,
With the twinkle of its candle
Lighting up the brakes and bushes,
And he sang the song of children,
Sang the song Nokomis taught him:
"Wah-wah-taysee, little firefly,
Little, flitting, white-fire insect,
Little, dancing, white-fire creature,
Light me with your little candle,
Ere upon my bed I lay me,
Ere in sleep I close my eyelids!"

Saw the moon rise from the water
Rippling, rounding from the water,
Saw the flecks and shadows on it,
Whispered, "What is that, Nokomis?"
And the good Nokomis answered:
"Once a warrior, very angry,
Seized his grandmother, and threw her
Up into the sky at midnight;
Right against the moon he threw her;
'Tis her body that you see there."

Saw the rainbow in the heaven,
In the eastern sky, the rainbow,
Whispered, "What is that, Nokomis?"
And the good Nokomis answered:
"'Tis the heaven of flowers you see there;
All the wild flowers of the forest,
All the lilies of the prairie,
When on earth they fade and perish
Blossom in that heaven above us."

When he heard the owls at midnight,
Hooting, laughing in the forest,
"What is that?" he cried in terror.
"What is that," he said, "Nokomis?"
And the good Nokomis answered:
"That is but the owl and owlet,
Talking in their native language,
Talking, scolding at each other."

Then the little Hiawatha
Learned of every bird its language,
Learned their names and all their secrets,
How they built their nests in Summer,
Where they hid themselves in Winter,
Talked with them whene'er he met them,
Called them "Hiawatha's Chickens."

Of all the beasts he learned the language,
Learned their names and all their secrets,
How the beavers built their lodges,
Where the squirrels hid their acorns,
How the reindeer ran so swiftly,
Why the rabbit was so timid,
Talked with them whene'er he met them,
Called them "Hiawatha's Brothers."

THE FLAG BEARER (FOR WILLIAM CARNEY OF COMPANY C)

CAROLE BOSTON WEATHERFORD

Across a sandy war-torn shore
the order came for the all-black corps
to charge Fort Wagner; take the lead;
muster courage for the deed.
Six hundred strong that scorching night
pushed ahead to spark the fight.
They marched as enemy fire rained,
a hail that left a bloody stain;
colonel, color-bearer, both struck down;
but the banner never touched the ground.
The flag, one soldier lifted high
toward the smoky summer sky,
crawling over windswept dunes,
dodging blasts despite his wounds.
The tattered flag would tell the story:
the Colored Troops' first stride to glory.

○

MOLLY PITCHER

KATE BROWNLEE SHERWOOD

'Twas hurry and scurry at Monmouth town,
    For Lee was beating a wild retreat;
The British were riding the Yankees down,
    And panic was pressing on flying feet.

Galloping down like a hurricane
    Washington rode with his sword swung high,
Mighty as he of the Trojan plain
    Fired by a courage from the sky.

"Halt, and stand to your guns!" he cried.
　　And a bombardier made swift reply.
Wheeling his cannon into the tide,
　　He fell 'neath the shot of a foeman nigh.

Molly Pitcher sprang to his side,
　　Fired as she saw her husband do.
Telling the king in his stubborn pride
　　Women like men to their homes are true.

Washington rode from the bloody fray
　　Up to the gun that a woman manned.
"Molly Pitcher, you saved the day,"
　　He said, as he gave her a hero's hand.

He named her sergeant with manly praise,
　　While her war-brown face was wet with tears—
A woman has ever a woman's ways,
　　And the army was wild with cheers.

◎

JOHN HENRY
AMERICAN FOLK SONG

John Henry was a very small boy,
Sitting on his mammy's knee;
He picked up a hammer and a little piece of steel,
Saying, "A hammer'll be the death of me, O Lord,
A hammer'll be the death of me."

John Henry went up on the mountain
And he came down on the side.
The mountain was so tall and John Henry was so small
That he laid down his hammer and he cried, "O Lord,"
He laid down his hammer and he cried.

John Henry was a man just six feet in height,
Nearly two feet and a half across the breast.
He'd take a nine-pound hammer and hammer all day long
And never get tired and want to rest, O Lord,
And never get tired and want to rest.

John Henry was a steel-driving man, O Lord,
He drove all over the world.
He come to Big Ben Tunnel on the C. & O. Road
Where he beat the steam drill down, O Lord,
Where he beat the steam drill down.

John Henry said to the captain,
"Captain, you go to town,
Bring me back a twelve-pound hammer
And I'll beat that steam drill down, O Lord,
And I'll beat that steam drill down."

They placed John Henry on the right-hand side,
The steam drill on the left;
He said, "Before I let that steam drill beat me down
I'll die with my hammer in my hand, O Lord,
And send my soul to rest."

The white folks all got scared,
Thought Big Bend was a-fallin' in;
John Henry hollered out with a very loud shout,
"It's my hammer a-fallin' in the wind, O Lord,
It's my hammer a-fallin' in the wind."

John Henry said to his shaker,
"Shaker, you better pray,
For if I miss that little piece of steel
Tomorrow'll be your buryin' day, O Lord,
Tomorrow'll be your buryin' day."

The man that invented that steam drill
He thought he was mighty fine.
John Henry sunk the steel fourteen feet
While the steam drill only made nine, O Lord,
While the steam drill only made nine.

John Henry said to his loving little wife,
"I'm sick and want to go to bed.
Fix me a place to lay down, Child;
There's a roarin' in my head, O Lord,
There's a roarin' in my head."

○

A SONG OF GREATNESS

CHIPPEWA INDIAN SONG
TRANSCRIBED BY MARY AUSTIN

When I hear the old men
Telling of heroes,
Telling of great deeds
Of ancient days,
When I hear them telling,
Then I think within me
I too am one of these.

When I hear the people
Praising great ones,
Then I know that I too
Shall be esteemed,
I too when my time comes
Shall do mightily.

Acknowledgments

Every effort has been made to locate all copyright holders. In the event that we have inadvertently omitted the proper notification, the editor would welcome hearing from the copyright holder and will take measures to amend subsequent editions accordingly. The publisher gratefully acknowledges the permission of the following publishers, estates, and individuals for their permission to reprint the poems listed.

"221st Chorus" by Jack Kerouac. Reprinted by permission of SLL Sterling Lord Literistic, Inc. Copyright © 1959 by Jack Keroauc.

"The Adventures of Isabel" by Ogden Nash, from *Nash's Pall Mall Magazine*. Copyright © 1936 by Ogden Nash. Reprinted by permission of Curtis Brown, Ltd.

"Afternoon with Grandmother," "The Library" by Barbara Huff, reprinted courtesy of the author.

"Archy, the Cockroach, Speaks," from *Archy and Mehitabel* by Don Marquis, copyright © 1927 by Doubleday, a division of Random House, Inc. Used by permission of Doubleday, a division of Random House, Inc.

"As I stared, he slowly changed," "It was when I was five years old," "Now I knew the sixth grandfather was about to speak," "Now suddenly there was nothing but a world of cloud" reprinted from *Black Elk Speaks: Being the Life Story of a Holy Man of the Oglala Sioux, The Premier Edition* by John G. Neihardt by permission of SUNY Press. Copyright © 1961 by the John G. Neihardt Trust. © 2008 by SUNY Press.

"Baby firefly," "Please, don't swat!," "A silent toad," "O wild goose" by Issa from *Cool Melons—Turn to Frogs!: The Life and Poems of Issa* by Matthew Golub. Text copyright © 1998 by Matthew Golub. Reprinted by permission of Lee & Low Books.

"Baby Running Barefoot" by D. H. Lawrence, from *The Complete Poems of D. H. Lawrence* by D. H. Lawrence, edited by V. de Sola Pinto & F. W. Roberts, copyright © 1964, 1971 by Angelo Ravagli and C. M. Weekley, Executors of the Estate of Frieda Lawrence Ravagli. Used by permission of Viking Penguin, a division of Penguin Group (USA) Inc.

"The Bad Kittens," "The Mouse," from *Compass Rose* by Elizabeth Coatsworth, copyright © 1929 by Coward-McCann, Inc., renewed © 1957 by Elizabeth Coatsworth. Used by permission of Coward-McCann, A Division of Penguin Young Readers Group, A Member of Penguin Group (USA) Inc., 3435 Hudson Street, New York, NY 10014. All rights reserved.

"A Bird came down the Walk," "The Brain is wider than the Sky," "Hope is the thing with feathers," "A narrow Fellow in the Grass," "There is no frigate like a book" by Emily Dickinson. Reprinted by permission of the publishers and the Trustees of Amherst College from *The Poems of Emily Dickinson*, Thomas H. Johnson, ed., Cambridge, Mass.: The Belknap Press of Harvard University Press, Copyright © 1951, 1955, 1979, 1983 by the President and Fellows of Harvard College.

"Blackberry Eating," "Daybreak," "Saint Francis and the Sow" from *Mortal Acts, Mortal Words* by Galway Kinnell. Copyright © 1980 by Galway Kinnell. Reprinted by permission of Houghton Mifflin Company. All rights reserved.

"A Blessing" by James Wright, in *The Branch Will Not Break* © 1963 by James Wright. Reprinted with the permission of Wesleyan University Press.

"Brown," "Hanukah Poem," "Thanksgiving Poem" by Arthur Green, reprinted courtesy of the author.

"The Cabalist" by Angelina Muñiz-Huberman, translated by Christine Deutsch, reprinted courtesy of the author.

"Cargoes," "Sea-Fever" by John Masefield reprinted by permission of The Society of Authors as the Literary Representative of the Estate of John Masefield.

"Chip the Glasses" and "Roads Go Ever Ever On" from *The Hobbit* by J. R. R. Tolkien. Copyright © 1966 by J. R. R. Tolkien. Copyright © renewed 1994 by Christopher R. Tolkien, John F. R. Tolkien and Priscilla M. A. R. Tolkien. Reprinted by permission of Houghton Mifflin Company. All rights reserved.

"Chrysalis Diary" by Paul Fleischman. Text copyright © 1988 by Paul Fleischman. Used by permission of HarperCollins Publishers.

"Friends" and "Pencils are my favorite friends" by Lou Lahr, reprinted courtesy of the author.

"The Gnome" from *Windy Morning* by Harry Behn. Copyright © 1953 by Harry Behn. Copyright renewed © 1981 by Alice Behn Goebel, Pamela Behn Adam, Prescott Behn, and Peter Behn. Used by permission of Marian Reiner.

"Good Sportsmanship" by Richard Armour, copyright © 1958 by Richard Armour. Reprinted by permission of John Hawkins & Associates, Inc. and Geoff Armour.

"The Grass on the Mountain " from *The American Rhythm* by Mary Austin. Copyright © 1930 by Mary Austin; copyright © renewed 1958 by Kenneth M. Chapman and Mary C. Wheelwright. "A Song of Greatness" from *The Children Sing in the Far West* by Mary Austin. Copyright © 1928 by Mary Austin; copyright © renewed 1956 by Kenneth M. Chapman and Mary C. Wheelwright. Reprinted by permission of Houghton Mifflin Harcourt Publishing Company. All rights reserved.

"Hiding," "Little" from *Here, There and Everywhere* by Dorothy Aldis, copyright © 1927, 1928, copyright renewed © 1955, 1956 by Dorothy Aldis. "Setting the Table" from *Any Spring* by Dorothy Aldis, copyright © 1933 renewed 1960 by Dorothy Aldis. Used by permission of G. P. Putnam's Sons, A Division of Penguin Young Readers Group, A Member of Penguin Group (USA) Inc., 345 Hudson Street, New York, NY 10014. All rights reserved.

"How To Tell Goblins from Elves," from *Goose Grass Rhymes* by Monica Shannon, copyright © 1930 by Doubleday, a division of Random House, Inc. Used by permission of Doubleday, a division of Random House, Inc.

"The Hunting Prayer" from *Hunting Sacred—Everything Listens* by Larry Littlebird. Copyright © 2001 by Larry Littlebird. Reprinted by permission of Western Edge Press.

"I Am Rose" by Gertrude Stein, from *The World Is Round* © 1938, 1939 by Gertrude Stein. Reprinted with the permission of the Estate of Gertrude Stein, through its Literary Executor, Mr. Stanford Gann, Jr. of Levin & Gann, P.A.

"Something Told the Wild Geese" by Rachel Field. Reprinted with the permission of Simon & Schuster Books for Young Readers, an imprint of Simon & Schuster Children's Publishing Division from *Poems* by Rachel Field. Copyright © 1934 by Macmillan Publishing Company; copyright renewed © 1962 by Arthur S. Pederson.

"The Song of the Jellicles" by T. S. Elliot, from *Old Possum's Book of Practical Cats*, copyright © 1939 by T. S. Elliot and renewed 1967 by Esme Valerie Eliot, reprinted by permission of Harcourt, Inc.

"Song of Man Chipping an Arrowhead" by W. S. Merwin, © 1973 by W. S. Merwin, permission of The Wylie Agency.

"Song of the Yeshiva Bocher" by Ahron Huebner, reprinted courtesy of the author.

"Thinking Time" from *City Kids* by Patricia Hubbell. Copyright © 2001 by Patricia Hubbell. Used by permission of Marian Reiner for the author.

"Timothy Winters," by Charles Causley, from *Collected Poems for Children* (Macmillan 2000). Reprinted by permission of David Higham Associates Limited.

"To P.J. (2 yrs old who sed write a poem for me in Portland, Oregon)" by Sonia Sanchez. Published in *It's a New Day* (Broadside Press, 1971, reprinted 1983), © 1971 Sonia Sanchez.

"Water night" by Octavio Paz, translated by Muriel Rukeyser, from *Early Poems 1935–1955*, copyright © 1973 by Octavio Paz and Muriel Rukeyser. Reprinted by permission of New Directions Publishing Corp.

"A Weak Poem (to be read lying down)" by Roger McGough from *Bad, Bad Cats* (© Roger McGough 1997) is reproduced by permission of PFD (www.pfd.co.uk) on behalf of Roger McGough.

"The wind blows out of the gates of the day" by William Butler Yeats. Reprinted with the permission of Scribner, a Division of Simon & Schuster, Inc., from *The Collected Plays of W. B. Yeats, Revised Edition* by William Butler Yeats. Copyright © 1934, 1052 by the Macmillan Publishing Company. Copyright renewed © 1962 by Bertha Georgie Yeats and 1980 by Anne Yeats. All rights reserved.

"Velvet Shoes," from *The Collected Poems of Elinor Wylie* by Elinor Wylie, copyright © 1932 by Alfred A. Knopf, a division of Random House, Inc., copyright © renewed 1960 by Edwina C. Rubenstein. Used by permission of Alfred A. Knopf, a division of Random House, Inc.

"When Young Melissa Sweeps" by Nancy B. Turner, from *Magpie Lane*, copyright © 1927 and renewed 1955 by Nancy Byrd Turner, reprinted by permission of Harcourt, Inc.

"Wynken, Blynken, and Nod" by Eugene Field. Reprinted with the permission of Atheneum Books for Young Readers, an imprint of Simon & Schuster Children's Publishing Division from *Poems of Childhood* by Eugene Field (New York, 1996).

"Young" from *All My Pretty Ones* by Anne Sexton. Copyright © 1962 by Anne Sexton, renewed 1990 by Linda G. Sexton. Reprinted by permission of Houghton Mifflin Company. All rights reserved.

"Your Catfish Friend" from *The Pill Versus the Springhill Mine Disaster* by Richard Brautigan. Copyright © 1968 by Richard Brautigan. Reprinted by permission of Houghton Mifflin Company. All rights reserved.

Index of First Lines

GREAT POEMS

in Just-, 126
In my craft or sullen art, 227
In the darkest winter nights, 135
In the shade I lie and ponder, 204
In winter I get up a night, 56
Ink runs from the corners of my mouth, 71
I once had a sweet little doll, dears, 40–41
I prithee, let me bring thee where crabs
      grow, 158
I quarreled with my brother, 36
Isabel met an enormous bear, 174–175
I saw a child. I said, "My boy," 84
I saw a Gnome, 149–150
I saw a proud, mysterious cat, 107–108
I saw a ship a-sailing, 9
I share a room, 35
I shot an arrow into the air, 85–86
I should like to rise and go, 204–205
"Is there anybody there?" said the
      Traveler, 156–157
"I think I want some pies this morning,"
      172–173
It looks like any building, 70
I, too, sing America, 193
It was many and many a year ago, 230–231
It was six men of Hindostan, 169–170
It was the wind that gave them life, 261
It was when I was five years old, 252
I used to speak, 33
I've known rivers, 243
I've often heard my mother say, 111
I wandered lonely as a cloud, 127–128
I went out to the hazel wood, 211–212
I went to the animal fair, 9
I will arise and go now, and go to
      Innisfree, 218
I woke before the morning, I was happy
      all the day, 57
I wonder, by my troth, what thou and I,
      226–227

J

Jack and Jill went up the hill, 11
Jack Sprat could eat no fat, 11

Jellicle Cats come out tonight, 17–18
Jenny kissed me when we met, 225
Jenny White and Johnny Black, 86
John Henry was a very small boy, 271–273
Joseph was an old man, 136
Just off the highway to Rochester,
      Minnesota, 118

L

Left, to the greenish, 89
"Let trees be made, for earth is bare," 239
Let us walk in the white snow, 139–140
Life is mostly froth and bubble, 162
Listen, my children, and you shall hear,
      182–185
Little children you will all go, 85
Little drops of water, 168
Little girl, be careful what you say, 83
Little Jack Horner, 3
Little Lamb, who made thee?, 239–240
A little nonsense now and then, 1
Little Orphant Annie's come to our house
      to stay, 50–51
The little Road says, Go, 218–219
The little songs of summer are all gone
      today, 130
Little things, that run, and quail, 121
A lone gray bird, 112
Long ago I learned how to sleep, 129
Look at you, magnificent creature lying
      there, 248
Look out! Look out, boys! Clear the track!,
      150
The Lord is my shepherd, 246
Love goes toward love, 222
Loveliest of trees, the cherry now, 125

M

maggie and milly and molly and may, 128
The man in the moon, 57
The man in the wilderness asked of me,
      12
Man was made for Joy & Woe, 167

Q

Quinquireme of Nineveh from distant
    Ophir, 216

R

Ride a cock horse, 5
Roads go ever ever on, 212–214

S

Said the Table to the Chair, 18–19
The saliva of a dragon, 144
'To see a world in a Grain of Sand, 113–114
The selfish shellfish, 6
Shall I compare thee to a summer's day?,
    229
She is a thistle-sifter, 5
She was a pretty little girl, 39–40
Shield yourselves against hell fire, 173
By the shores of Gitchee Gumee, 267–
    269
A sign was leaning toward adobe shacks,
    87
A silent toad, 104
Simple and fresh and fair from winter's
    close emerging, 127
Sing a song of sixpence, 10–11
Sing unto the Lord with Thanksgiving, 124
"Sister, sister, go to bed," 34–35
Six little mice sat down to spin, 10
Skimming an asphalt sea, 79
Sleep, my child, and peace attend thee, 59
So I say to you, my friends, 194–195
Some hae meat and canna eat, 43
Someone came knocking, 155
Something told the wild geese, 133
Sometimes I like to be alone, 38
Sometimes when I don't want to go,
    38–39
Sometimes when we go out for walks, 34
So, naturalists observe, a flea, 5
Soon Shabbat will be here, 42
So, that's how it's going to be, 114–115

Speak gently, Spring, and make no sudden
    sound, 111–112
The sun was shining on the sea, 22–25
Sweet are the uses of adversity, 162

T

Teach your children, 247
There is no frigate like a book, 211
There lived a sage in days of yore, 15
There's snow on the fields, 52
There was a child went forth every day,
    92–94
There was a crooked man, 10
There was a little girl, 39
There was an old woman tossed up in a
    basket, 2
There was an owl lived in an oak, 4
There were three gypsies a-come to my
    door, 231–232
They went to sea in a Sieve, they did,
    208–210
The things, good Lord, that we pray for,
    171
This land is your land, 200
A thousand doors ago, 260–261
Three little kittens lost their mittens,
    7–8
Timmy and Tommy and Toby and me,
    206–208
Timothy Winters comes to school, 88–89
'Tis the voice of a sluggard; I hear him
    complain, 171
Today my mama, 33
Today, picking up a book, 69
To-day's your natal day, 41
Tomás you are a liar, 85
To try to say it, 36
'Twas brillig, and the slithy toves, 14
'Twas hurry and scurry at Monmouth
    town, 270–271
Twinkle, twinkle, little star, 242
Two roads diverged in a yellow wood,
    214
Tyger! Tyger! burning bright, 240–241

Index of Authors

GREAT POEMS

Index of Titles

GREAT POEMS